Home Seller's Bible

For: Home Owners, Agents & Investors

2019

MULTI-AWARD WINNING AUTHOR & REALTOR

MARK E. MEINCKE

Contributing Authors:

Julie Boake, Larry Metz, Robyn Ross, Cory Alger, James C. Lozinsky, Shawna Roch, Sandi Scott, Nathan Prins, Bernice Winter, Troy Niemans

Printed in Canada

ISBN 978-1-9994343-0-4

FIN 29 10 2018

Contents

Introduction v

1. Chicken or the Egg? 1

2. Am I Selling / Buying a Home, an Investment Property... or Both? 6

3. Building Wealth with an Investment Property 10

4. Buying and Selling in a Declining Market 19

5. Revenue is Vanity, Profit is Sanity 21

6. The Right Financing Option for My Needs, *by Sandi Scott* 23

7. The Price is Right! (How to Properly Price Your Home) 34

8. How Much Should I Offer When I'm Buying? 54

9. You Can Skip Breakfast, But Do NOT Skip a Home Inspection, *by Robyn Ross* 60

10. Legal Landmines, *by James C. Lozinsky LLP* 73

11. The Case for the RPR, *by Nathan Prins* 94

12. What is Mortgage Fraud and How Does it Affect Me? 100

13. Pre-Sale Renovations and R.O.I. (Dumb Money vs Smart Money) 106

14. Roofing Rescue, *by Larry Metz* 114

15. Top 8 "Must Knows" on Flooring, *by Cory Alger* 119

16. Home Staging Essentials 133

17. Major Marketing Mistakes 136

18. Social Media Matters, *by Julie Boake* 139

19. The LOVE Meter 145

20. Showing Your Home to Potential Buyers –
How NOT to Do It (For Both Agents and Owners) 149

21. Common Real Estate Myths 154

22. Crucial Negotiation Skills and Tactics 156

23. Responding to a Purchase Offer 165

24. Realtor Commissions are 100% Negotiable...
Yes Really! 173

25. Disloyalty Can Be Costly for Investors 180

26. The Secret Truth About "Commission Free"
For-Sale-By-Owner Companies and
Discount Realtors 182

27. Personal Safety / Security While Selling / Buying 192

28. Rent To Own Myths and Misconceptions,
by Shawna Roch 197

29. Digging Yourself Out of the Rental Rut 207

30. Buying and Selling Condominium Property
in Alberta, *by Bernice Winter ACCI, FCCI,
founder of Condo-Check* 212

31. Water Wells, *by Troy Niemans* 239

32. Septic Systems, *by Troy Niemans* 249

33. Home Water Systems, *by Troy Niemans* 262

Introduction

In the beginning, there was chaos.

The wealthy took advantage of average property owners by over-charging when they sold to them, and under-paying when they bought from them. Homeowners didn't have access to the information they needed, which would allow them to develop an understanding of property values, nor did they have the savvy to navigate the property transfer process safely. Great wealth was transferred from the poor to the rich, with no obvious recourse for the average property owner.

And then...an industry was created.

The National Association of REALTORS® was founded as the National Association of Real Estate Exchanges on May 12, 1908 in Chicago. The National Association of Real Estate Exchanges' objective was "to unite the real estate professionals of America for the purpose of effectively exerting a combined influence upon matters affecting real estate interests." (source: www.nar.realtor.com) Finally, there was a resource to both protect and advocate for the average person.

And then...there was light!

Realtor Mark Meincke and ten other industry professionals have stepped up to provide the public with the ground-breaking HOME SELLERS BIBLE. The Home Seller's Bible pulls back the curtain for both home sellers, and aspiring home buyers, providing an "insiders" look at the world of Real Estate.

Whether you are selling by owner or with the help of a professional Realtor, this book can help you to STOP LOSING THOUSANDS of dollars.

1

Chicken or the Egg? "Should I Buy Before My Home is Sold?"

If you already own a home and you're considering a move, it's only natural to start shopping before you sell your primary residence. Touring show homes, open houses, and the MLS™ to look before you leap can be exciting and fun... but beware. Let me share a true story of home sellers who decided to buy a new home before their current home was sold.

During the great market rise and fall of 2007-2008, homeowners were relishing in their newfound wealth. Their home equity was skyrocketing by about ten thousand dollars a month, allowing them to take out home lines of credit to buy all kinds of RVs and toys, take dream trips, and drive brand new cars. We thought the ride would never end... but of course it did in a catastrophic fashion. Clients of mine were living in Morinville, just north of Edmonton. I had sold them the home in 2006 at a great price, but during the rise of 2007, they decided to move another two hours north to be closer to family. Before I listed their home, they started looking at homes in the area they were planning to move to. Knowing how dangerous this could be, I strongly urged them to NOT buy, and NOT make an offer prior to the sale of their current home. Despite my pleas for patience, they fell in love with a home during a strong seller's market, and they purchased the home with a 90 day possession. Now, we were under the gun. They didn't realize at the time, but they had purchased the home one week after the market had peaked, and their primary residence was already starting to depreciate at a staggering pace. They now had to sell in a buyer's market, after they had just bought in a seller's market, meaning a loss of tens of thousands of dollars. When we listed the home, I explained the declining trend and how we had to stay ahead of the curve in order to sell. Again, they did not heed my advice when I urged a reasonable asking price. Instead, they instructed me to list the home for more than it was worth... just in case the "right buyer" came along. Every week I would show them the new market stats, urging them to adjust the price accordingly, and every week they would refuse. Two months later, the home was not sold and they were in really bad shape. An investor came along with a terrible offer which they were forced to accept because they couldn't afford two mortgages and didn't qualify for the new mortgage without first selling their home. ***Their total loss was roughly $80,000.00****. For a* *young couple with a modest income, this was a large fortune to lose.*

The moral of the story is.... SELL FIRST, BUY AFTER.

I concede that the circumstances of this story are extreme; however, even in a balanced market, you can expect to easily lose $10,000.00 - $20,000.00 if you choose to buy before you sell.

Here is why:

One of the worst conditions you can put on a purchase offer is ***"subject to the sale of the buyer's home"***. In reality, this isn't even a true offer, it's more of a "notice of intent" than a valid offer to purchase, and any good listing agent will advise their client as such. Due to presenting a weak and unattractive offer, you are nearly guaranteed to pay far more for the home than if you were to write a strong and attractive offer. If your offer is accepted, you are now under pressure to sell your home, and are vulnerable to accepting poor offers because you are under the gun.

The bottom line is, if you buy before you sell, you'll be in a weak bargaining position... TWICE. On a home worth between $300,000.00 and 500,000.00, you can easily expect to lose between $10,000.00 to $20,000.00 or more due to a lack of negotiation power. For homes over $500,000.00, that number grows proportionally. Whenever possible, you always want to put yourself into a strong bargaining position and avoid being in a position of weakness. Bargaining power matters, and is often worth tens of thousands of dollars per transaction.

Section Notes

What was my greatest take-away from this section?

What do I need to remember about this section?

2

Am I Selling / Buying a Home, Investment Property or Both?

Most Realtors® and sophisticated Real Estate investors look at their personal home from a different perspective than the average homeowner. Though they still wish to have a pleasant home which is a fit for their family, they also consider issues which affect both the resale factors and the equity accretion potential of the property.

When either buying or selling your home, it pays to be aware of both current and trending market factors which affect the value accretion potential of your property in comparison to other properties.

A few of the key factors to consider are:

- Desirability / Rarity of location
- If you are on or near a green-belt, is it temporary or permanent?

- If you have a great view, is there new construction in the future which will possibly destroy or obstruct the view?
- Are you either facing or near a through road?
- Are you on an outside corner lot? If so, do you have a sidewalk around the entire street perimeter?
- Is the location down-wind from a source of unpleasant odours?
- How many rentals are in the immediate neighbourhood?
- Are the neighbours loud and rowdy?
- Past, current and potential future crime rates based on current trend forecasting
- High crime centres nearby, such as dodgy hotels, or a park which is frequented by criminals or drug addicts
- Reputation of the School District
- Density of rush hour traffic to and from that location
- Current market attitude of the house design features (e.g.: sunken living room)
- Is the floor plan attractive to most buyers who are interested in that area?
- Cost of required renovations
- Do the required renovations represent a potential loss or will they provide an R.O.I. (Return On Investment)?
- How much of an R.O.I. can you expect from the required renovations?
- Bargaining position of the seller
- How many homes are on the market in that area compared to other areas?
- Historical reputation of the area (stigma)

- Desirability of the style of home
- Local, Provincial, National and International Economic factors
- Current fair market value
- Current and projected mortgage rates
- Current and projected mortgage lending rules
- Quality and style of the finishing
- Quality of commuting from that location
- Public Transit

Depending on the criteria and strategy you choose for your home sale or purchase, you can either lose tens of thousands of dollars or you can gain tens of thousands of dollars. Not to say that profit should be your biggest factor, but the more of a factor you make it, the more wealth you may create by simply making smart choices during the sales process.

KNOW YOUR MARKET!

When you are purchasing solely from the perspective of "a great home for our family", many of the above considerations certainly apply as well. However, many home buyers / sellers don't factor in as many considerations as they should prior to selling or buying. The bottom line is, you CAN have your cake and eat it too if you're patient and diligent in your choices. You can have a great home for your family, which also happens to be a savvy investment property as well.

Section Notes

What was my greatest take-away from this section?

What do I need to remember about this section?

3

Building Wealth With an Investment Property

If you're starting out as a First Time Home Buyer (FTHB), you can become an investor with your very first purchase. It's easiest if you're single or if you don't have any children, but even with a family you can use this formula. Here's one way to build your wealth with Real Estate.

1. Buy a home which has a separate suite, and live in the suite while renting out the rest of the home.

2. Every cent of rent which you collect, put into a separate account... never touch it.

3. Once the balance is enough for a down payment on your next property, buy another home with a suite and move into the next home while renting out your previous suite.

4. Repeat, repeat, repeat, as much as you can, as fast as you can.

Each home you purchase cuts your first mortgage time in half. By the time you have your fifth home, you will have so much equity that you will be the equivalent of mortgage free on your first home.

Your first ten years are the hardest, but the second ten years are when the mortgages get paid off faster, as more is put on the principle. By the time 20-25 years are gone, you will be mortgage free on at least four properties and can easily retire by living off of the rental revenue.

If you have kids, the same formula applies, only you'll likely want to live in the main part of the home and rent out the basement or secondary suite. The trick is to NOT touch the rental income. Save every nickel of it, and only use it as money for a down payment on your next property. This is easier said than done, but the more disciplined you are, the quicker you will build your wealth.

An average person with an average income can retire in their 40s with a net worth well north of a million dollars by simply following this plan. It's not easy, but it is simple.

The greatest challenge is coping with nightmare tenants. I've had them all. From destructive squatters to an amazing family who did renovations on my property then refused to charge me. I've dealt with tenants who couldn't change a light bulb on their own, and have had tenants who refinished the hardwood. Regardless of the type of tenant you end up with, the common thread is to keep the relationship as positive as possible with them. If your relationship goes south, it will cost you money every time.

An angry tenant can:

- Possibly stay for up to an extra 90 days without paying rent
- Trash the place as they move out
- Consistently pay the rent late
- Do a midnight move and hand the keys to their "friends" who become squatters
- Leave behind mountains of garbage
- Destroy flooring
- Incur thousands of dollars in damages which you will never recover from them... ever
- Call you at all hours of the night, falsely claiming the furnace went out
- Adopt a huge dog, regardless of whether or not you have pet restrictions
- Make owning an investment property a nightmare and not worth the headache

A Happy Tenant can:

- Consistently pay the rent on time
- Only call you for help if there is a true emergency
- Keep the home clean and in good repair
- Abide by the terms of the tenancy agreement

- Offer to purchase the home when you are ready to sell
- Make owning an investment property a dream come true and the best investment ever

It's in your best interest to treat tenants as valuable clients, not as subordinates. In fact, you may even wish to change the title of the Tenancy Agreement to "Client Agreement".

You are providing a service for someone who is paying for that service, which makes the tenant a client. Too often, landlords take their tenants for granted or even abuse them. The tenants are in a position to make life miserable for you if they wish to, and should be treated with due care.

To ensure the best chances of having a positive client relationship with your tenant, there are two types of measures to take:

1. Preventative legal measures and tenant selection
2. Scheduled relationship maintenance

In your tenant / client agreement, you should have a section which outlines credit reporting. Not all tenants care about their credit score, but most do. If a tenant is late paying or fails to pay rent, the threat of credit reporting provides the landlord with valuable leverage.

When screening potential clients / tenants, you may wish to do a credit check. If there is a couple moving in, it's best to run a credit check on both of them.

When deciding who to have as a client, give strong consideration to which stage of their life they are in and what the trend is with their life. Are they an ambitious young couple who are both fresh out of University or trade school? Are they in their 30s with a total lack of direction in their life? The best tenants are stable and have a clear path in front of them.

How long do they typically stay in a home? It's important to know their rental history because if they have a habit of moving every six months, there is a high likelihood they will maintain that trend and be moving out as fast as they move in.

Have they owned in the past and plan to own again? If so, the chances are they will be fantastic tenants. Life happens, and sometimes you hit a rocky road. My family has lost it all... twice. In both instances, we went from being homeowners to being tenants. As tenants, we always paid on time and left the home in better condition than we found it. Eventually we got back on our feet and became homeowners again. The best tenants I've ever had were in the same boat and are now landlords themselves, owning numerous properties.

Scheduled relationship maintenance

Client relationship maintenance means that you remember important dates such as their "move in date" or their kid's birthdays. If that's too much, just drop off a pumpkin at Halloween and cookies at Christmas. Let them know you are happy to have them and that they matter to you.

Twice a year provide them with a "Satisfaction Survey". Instead of performing a formal inspection of the property (which is done discreetly when you drop off the cookies and pumpkins), provide them with a Satisfaction Survey to make sure they are content with both the home and their tenant relationship. This will make them feel valued and uncover any potential issues they may have.

The survey may look something like this:

Please answer the following six questions
using a scale of 1-5.

1. Very unsatisfied **2.** Somewhat unsatisfied
3. Meh... no comment **4.** Satisfied **5.** Very satisfied

a. The physical condition of my home ______
b. My neighbours ______
c. My neighbourhood ______
d. My landlord ______
e. The cost of my rent ______
f. The cost of my utilities ______

Please circle your answer:

How much longer do you plan to stay at this residence?

1. Less than a year?

2. Less than 2 years?

3. Less than 3 years?

4. Less than 4 years?

Would you like to purchase your own property at some point? Yes / No

If YES, would you purchase a property right away if you were approved for financing today? Yes / No

If YES, would you like some help or recommendations for getting pre-approved for a mortgage? Yes / No

If YES, would you like a Realtor to contact you to help you find a great home of your own? Yes / No

What can be done to make your experience living here even better?

The yes / no questions might seem a bit odd to ask, but there is a reason for asking them. Tenants fear being evicted, and to protect themselves they are less likely to be honest if they are fearful. These questions are designed to make it less threatening to be honest. The data is only useful to you if it's accurate. You may wish to consider having this survey anonymous or using a third party agency to collect the data for you.

If you own a property management company, the answers to these questions will help you forecast upcoming vacancy rates so you can be prepared. If you only have one property, the honest answers to these questions will still help you be prepared and help you avoid being surprised by a suddenly vacant property.

Whether it's good news or bad news, it is important for landlords to be "in the know" so they are not blindsided. The vast majority of landlords are reactionary, but it doesn't have to be that way.

Section Notes

What was my greatest take-away from this section?

What do I need to remember about this section?

4

Buying / Selling In a Declining Market

If the market starts to fall, don't panic. Here are your best three options on how to react to a falling market.

Option #1. Stay put

This is your worst option, and it requires a great deal of patience. Markets rise and fall, and unless you bought at an unusually high market peak, your home value will return eventually. While you still have equity in your home, now would be a good time to acquire an additional property for investment purposes. Just make sure you are acquiring a property which has a great potential for both renovation ROI, as well as future cash flow. The difficulty is knowing where you are in the market slide and guessing where the bottom will be. It's fine to wait until the market hits bottom, but only if you will still have enough leverage from the equity in your current home as either collateral or to secure a line of credit for the down payment.

Option #2. Sell... wait... buy

This can be a very profitable option, but can also be the most difficult because of the waiting part. You never know when the market will stop falling, so you could sell your home right before the market stabilizes. If this occurs, you'll need a place to stay until you have successfully found a great deal.

The longer you can wait, the better the deal you will get when you buy. If an interim residence is out of the question, negotiate the longest possession date you can for your own home. Just make sure you have received a large deposit on the sale of your home to ensure the buyers aren't tempted to back out of the deal and lose the deposit. The bottom line here is sell high, buy low.

Option #3. Rent out your existing home... wait... buy

This way you don't lose any equity as a result of selling costs; however, you will still lose equity in your home as the market is falling. Again, the trick is in the waiting. It's tough to know when you're at the bottom of the market or how long the market will stay at the bottom.

5

Revenue is Vanity, Profit is Sanity

Selling a home is an expensive process no matter how you look at it. Some of the expenses which people are surprised by may include:

- Updating your RPR (Real Property Report)
- Doing a pre-inspection
- Pre-sale renovations
- Decluttering
- Staging
- Storage
- Movers
- Realtor fees (if you use one)
- FSBO company fees
- Advertising / marketing
- Taking time off work

- Entertaining your family while you vacate your home to allow for showings. E.g.: meals, movies, activities, gas, aggravation
- **MORTGAGE PENALTIES**
- Mail forwarding
- New utility and internet hookups
- Paying out the security company contract
- And on, and on, and on

All of a sudden, this big windfall of money you THOUGHT you were getting is considerably smaller than what you were counting on. The sale of your home is a business transaction and must be looked at as such.

Create a P&L (Profit and Loss) sheet for your home, and subtract the loss from the gross profit to find your NET profit. Once you see how much smaller that number is, you might make different choices with your pre-sale expenditures.

6

The Right Financing Option for Me

by Sandi Scott

Disclaimer: The rules have changed and will continue to change after this book is published. Everything I am about to share with you is based on the Alberta market as of June 2018.

I often find that when I am introducing myself at a networking event, I say, "Mortgages aren't fun, but I am" and it always gets a laugh. It's true, although mortgages aren't the most exciting topic, most of us will have at least one mortgage in our lifetime, so it's a great idea to be well informed.

Let's start with the basic components of your mortgage:

- Rate
- Term
- Amortization

- Prepayment options
- Payout penalties

Although there is a lot more to your mortgage than just rate, this is almost always my clients' first question and concern. In years past in the mortgage industry, "What is your best rate?" used to be a straightforward question to answer. Now, it is a far more convoluted process. High ratio (insured) or conventional? Meaning, what will your down payment be? If you put any less than 20% of the purchase price as your down payment, your mortgage is considered "high ratio" and you will have to pay mandatory government insurance, commonly known as a CMHC fee, although this is only one of the three mortgage insurers. The other two are Genworth and Canada Guaranty.

The insurance fee is a percentage of your total mortgage amount. This percentage is also based on the percentage of your down payment to purchase price, commonly known as the "Loan To Value" or LTV.

Your mortgage is considered conventional if you put 20% or more as your down payment. In this case, there is no mortgage insurance required or the insurance is paid by the lender internally. The insurance percentage calculations are also different for a revenue property versus an owner-occupied property.

As you can see, all the variables mentioned above plus several other factors such as credit score, type of income,

etc. means that quoting a rate in today's lending environment is near impossible without knowing more details about your individual situation.
Next, we have the types of rates:

- A fixed rate stays the same over the term of the mortgage
- A variable rate changes with the current prime rate

Both have their pros and cons. When choosing a fixed rate, clients feel more comfortable knowing that their rate will remain the same for the term of their mortgage. Clients who are comfortable with a little more risk may choose a variable rate, with the hope that the prime rate will remain lower and they will save money over the term. With a variable rate mortgage, you can lock into your lender's fixed rate at any time if you take a term equal to or greater than the term remaining on your current mortgage. Statistics show that, historically, mortgage holders have saved more on a variable rate.

Then we have the term of your mortgage. This can range from one to five years. Generally, a five year term is the most popular. Usually the reason for this is that people feel more comfortable knowing their rate will not change for five years. Also, it is easier to maintain a predictable budget with a five year term.

The amortization period of a mortgage is the amount of time it will take you to pay off your entire mortgage. In other words, the number of years your payments are spread over. Generally, the standard amortization period for a new mortgage is 25 years. With the current mortgage rules, if your down payment is 20% or more, you can go up to a 30 year amortization with certain lenders.

There are pros and cons to shorter and longer amortization. An advantage of amortizing over a longer period is that your monthly payments will be lower. A disadvantage is that you will pay more interest over the total period. With a shorter amortization period, your payments will be larger, but you will pay less interest over the entire length of the mortgage. In below examples, we are using a $300,000.00 mortgage with a five year fixed rate of 3.49%. You can see that, although increasing the amortization up to 30 years reduces the payments by about $155.00 a month, you do end up paying more interest and less towards the principal at the end of the term.

Another concern for clients is, "How much prepayment does the mortgage allow?" In other words, "How much extra money can I pay on my mortgage without incurring a penalty?"

To answer, this differs from lender to lender. The general amount is 20% of the current mortgage balance per calendar year, although some lenders are 15% and some may be only 10%. This factor could definitely be of consideration if you are someone who receives larger bonuses or lump sum payments through their employment each year and you wish to pay down a portion of your mortgage in this way. If feasible, it is a great idea to make extra payments on your mortgage, as these amounts go directly towards your principal and can decrease your amortization – how long it will take to pay your mortgage off – greatly.

As an example, using a $300,000.00 mortgage at a 3.49% five year fixed rate, if you paid a $10,000.00 lump sum each year for five years, you would decrease your amortization by over five years and reduce your interest considerably.

The payout penalties also differ with a fixed and variable rate mortgage. With a fixed rate mortgage, if you wish to pay out your mortgage early or payout more than is allowed as a prepayment (generally 15% or 20% of the mortgage balance), you will be subject to an IRD (Interest Rate Differential). This is the difference in interest between your mortgage rate and the lender's current interest rate of the term closest to the remaining term of your mortgage. This is so the lender does not lose out on any interest repayment on those funds.

See example below:
You have a balance of $300,000.00 left on your mortgage, your remaining term is 26 months and your current interest rate is 3.49%. The lender's rate of their closet term (24 months) is 3.29%. Your payout penalty will be the difference between 3.49% and 3.29%, so you will be charged 0.20% of the current balance for the remainder of the term, 26 months.

Also, the rate used to calculate your interest rate differential is not always the same from lender to lender. Generally, the banks use their posted rates for the calculations, whereas our non-bank / monoline mortgage lenders use their best rate. This can result in a vast difference, and the bank's IRD will often be considerably higher. It is a very prudent idea to ensure that you fully understand this process before you proceed with your mortgage. This is where your trusted Mortgage Broker will guide and advise you.

The role of a Mortgage Broker

You may ask yourself, what is the role of a Mortgage Broker and why wouldn't I just go directly to my bank to borrow money to purchase a home?

It is a surprising fact but many people are still unclear of the role of a Mortgage Broker. As a Mortgage Broker, I am often asked, "Oh, you sell houses?" Actually, I don't, but oftentimes that is the perception.

As a Mortgage Broker, I assist you in finding the best financing for the biggest purchase of your life – your home. I do not take this responsibility lightly and make every single client my highest priority.

My favourite client to deal with is the first-time home buyer. It is so amazing helping someone get into their first home, guiding them through the process step-by-step and watching them achieve the dream of their first home purchase! I deal directly with your Realtor, your appraiser and your lawyer to make the process as seamless as possible for you.

I am often told, "You made it so easy!" and that makes me very happy! I have been very fortunate to help many friends' children purchase their homes and this is so rewarding.

Five reasons to use a Mortgage Broker:

1. Our services are free to the client as we are paid by the lender. The only exception to this is if we need to source out untraditional or private financing, as this may incur a fee.

2. Generally, we can obtain better rates for you as we have access to many, many different financial institutions. We provide millions of dollars worth of business to these lenders each year and they pass on their deepest discounts to us, for you.

3. We do all the legwork for you. One call to a Mortgage Broker is the same as numerous calls to different banks and lenders. We even use the same credit bureau for all our lenders to save multiple enquiries on your bureau.

4. We come to you! We can get all your financing done in the comfort of your own home, saving you time and travel.

5. We will maintain contact with you through the term of your mortgage, reviewing your mortgage and advising you of ways you may be able to save money as you go. When your term is up, we'll give you free, professional advice on whether you should renew with your current lender or whether there's a better situation elsewhere at that time.

Switching/transferring a mortgage

Frequently, people get into a mortgage and feel they have to stay in that same mortgage for the full term. It is always a good idea to get a "mortgage check-up" every once in a while to see if that is still the best mortgage for you. The common perception is that it will cost you too much to payout your mortgage, even if you see a lower rate somewhere else. I find many times when I'm chatting with someone and tell them what I do, they say, "My mortgage doesn't come due until..." When I ask what kind of rate they have, they often say, "I'm not sure, but I don't think it's that good..." I then suggest that it may be a smart idea to revisit it. Many times, the interest you will save over time with your new rate will more than compensate for any penalty you may have to pay to get out of the original mortgage. Also, many lenders pay all legal fees if you switch your mortgage to them, and some will also add the penalty, or a portion of it, to your new mortgage balance so it doesn't come directly out of your pocket.

Renewing your mortgage

Another common misconception among mortgage holders is that you have to renew with your current lender when you receive their renewal notice. Generally, the rate that is offered to you at renewal is not one of the best rates. It pays to shop around.

This is an optimal time to contact a Mortgage Broker to see if they can find you a better rate with a different financial institution.

Reverse mortgage

A large number of seniors have built up significant equity in their home over the years but have a minimal monthly income. A Reverse Mortgage is an excellent product that allows people who are 55+ to access up to 55% of the equity in their homes. The beauty of this product is that these individuals do not have to qualify for this mortgage and do not have to make monthly payments. The loan only comes due when the property is sold.

As a homeowner with a reverse mortgage, you are always in control and the property title remains in your name. The reverse mortgage is structured so you can choose how you wish to receive your money. You can receive it as a lump sum payment or in monthly payments, whichever suits your needs.

This can be a very handy resource for seniors who wish to use some of the equity in their home for things like travel, paying medical expenses, paying off debt or lending money to their children or grandchildren.

As you can see, when you are making the largest purchase of your life, it is extremely important to speak with an expert to advise you of all your options and help you navigate the process. A Mortgage Broker works for you and is generally more specialized than your contact at the bank since mortgages are all we do!

Section Notes

What was my greatest take-away from this section?

What do I need to remember about this section?

7

The Price is Right! (How to Properly Price Your Home)

Do you have kids? If so, when they were first born, did anyone come up to you and say, "Whoa! That is one ugly baby!"? I'm guessing... probably not. Your child is the centre of your universe, and couldn't be more beautiful. When you've lived in a home for years, done renovations and maintained it, most people create a bond with their home whether they realize it or not. Your home becomes your baby. This bond makes it difficult to price the home objectively.

When you own an investment property, the equity becomes your baby. You know every cent you've invested, the mortgage balance, and how many times you had to tend to the tenants needs at all hours of the night. When you go to sell this property, rest assured it is STILL your baby and your ability to remain objective is almost certainly impaired.

Most times, when I look at comparable properties with sellers, they cherry pick poor comparables then pitch me on why the expensive comparables best represent their home. It's a natural impulse to cherry pick the numbers you want to see, and it's my job to help my clients be realistic and honest when interpreting the comparable properties. Some home sellers are easier to reason with than others, and most times I'm able to sober up my clients with a healthy dose of reality... but not always.

If you're selling on your own, the common practice is to take advantage of the common Realtors offer for "FREE HOME EVALUATIONS!" I encourage you to take full advantage of the offer and to collect three evaluations from three different Realtors. What you'll find is you'll get different advice from different perspectives, but you'll also get critical information you'll need in order to make your decision.

CAUTION, SOME REALTORS MAY NOT BE 100% HONEST

I hurts me to admit it, but it's true. Not all of us are created equal. About twice a month I receive a notice from the Real Estate Council of Alberta (RECA) that yet another Realtor has been fined or has lost their license for life due to breaking our strict Code of Conduct. Out of roughly 5000 Realtors, that's not so bad, but it's still embarrassing to me and to most of us who run a clean business.

Here is what to look out for if you're getting a "Free home evaluation" from a total stranger.

1. Sunshine being blown up your butt

In Realtor speak, we call it "buying a listing". Some Realtors play on your natural greed, and promise you the moon and stars for the potential selling price, only to come back to you two months later and say, "Darn it! The market has shifted and we need to drop the price by at least $20,000.00!" This is a tactic that I deplore, but I've seen it work many times.

In situations where there are multiple Realtors competing for a listing, some Realtors feel pressured to inflate their recommended selling price, knowing that if they are the only ones to tell the truth, chances are they will not win the listing.

The injury to the seller can be significant because the listing often gets stigmatized as having "unreasonable sellers" and buyers simply avoid even viewing it. The property then becomes a "stale listing" which rarely sells. Even if it does sell, you'll be getting BOTTOM DOLLAR for your home for no other reason than your choice of marketing strategy.

Even if you never lower your price, some Realtors still love to have listings because listings are the best source of advertising, and often result in securing new clients. It is plausible that some Realtors may be tempted to consistently list really high to ensure your home DOESN'T sell fast because it may be more important for the Realtor to collect the leads generated by the listing rather than selling the listing itself. In a slow market, the temptation can be even greater.

2. High pressure listing tactics

I've taken several "Realtor Success Courses" over the years, and sadly many of them still use the tired, old, ugly tactics which went out of style in the 1980s.

If you let an old school "Wolf of Real Estate" in your home, it's neither easy nor comfortable to get them out. An average market evaluation should consist of providing you with the information you need and answering your questions. If you feel pressured to cancel all your other appointments for market evaluations or to list NOW, then it's time to show that Realtor the door. When you list your home with a Realtor, it should be with someone you're not only confident in but comfortable with as well.

3. The low ball

This tactic is less popular, but it does happen. Some Realtors are more concerned with a quick, easy sale than getting the seller every possible penny for their home. When these types present you with a market evaluation, they cherry pick all the lowest prices then try to convince you why your home is very comparable to these homes. This leaves the seller with less money in their pocket than they deserve.

Sold vs active listings

When evaluating your home value based on the comparable properties in your area, be sure to put 90% of your focus on the properties which actually SOLD. If you put more than 10% of your focus on the active listings, you will be basing your decision on properties that may be overpriced. To successfully sell your home, you have to compare it to other homes which have successfully SOLD. It's also valuable to look at the listings that have expired, which provides you with the information on how NOT to price your home. Current active listings give you an idea as to your competition, and they do play a role in the decision making; however, neither banks nor professional appraisers pay any attention to any property other than those which have successfully SOLD. It's wise to follow their example.

Your "go to market" strategy

Beware of "Market Tests"

It's common for people who don't really HAVE to sell to put their home on the market for a little more than they know it's worth just in case the right buyer comes along. The term for this tactic is a "Market Test". It's a silly term, as the Market is very predictable and doesn't really need to be tested. I admit, however, every once in a blue moon sellers do get lucky with this strategy and get top dollar for their home. If you're going to play this lottery, you better have a home which is both a rare find and highly attractive in your market or the market test is almost certain to prove that your price is simply too high.

If you take the gamble of starting too high and you lose the bet, the consequence of losing is that both you and your home get stigmatized. You personally get stigmatized as being an unreasonable seller, and your home gets stigmatized as being unattractive. Neither of these stigmatization may be true, however, the market perception will still be negative all the same. This stigma increases the possibility that your home may become what's commonly referred to as a stale listing, and stale listings usually morph into an expired listing. The bottom line is that not only does your home not sell, but you should keep it off the market for at least six months before you put it back on again in order to give the stigma a chance to wear off.

You may ask, "Can't I just reduce the price?" The short answer is yes, of course you can, however, when buyers see a significant price reduction, the impression they get is that you won't be willing to negotiate much further because you have already dropped the price by a significant amount. The net result is that buyers are STILL discouraged from even viewing your property if you started too high.

In most cases, if you ask too much to start off with, you will usually receive a lower selling price than if you priced your home correctly from the beginning.

What is a COMPARABLE property?

When comparing your home to others, it's best to start looking in your immediate neighbourhood for other homes which have recently sold, are the same style of home, similar in age, similar in condition and similar in size. For good science, you're going to want to have detailed information on least six to ten good comparable properties for you to make an informed decision on how to price your home.

Often you will struggle to get enough comparable properties in your immediate neighbourhood, so the next step is to pull comparables from similar neighbourhoods until you've collected at least six to choose from.

Apples to apples

You should only directly compare a **two-storey** with an attached garage to other two stories with attached garages. Two stories with detached garages are in their own category, as buyers usually prefer one or the other.

Bungalows, however, can be compared to **bi-levels**, but not to **semi-bungalows**. Bi-levels are best compared to **raised bungalows**, as both have large basement windows. Walk-out bungalows / bi-levels are in a separate category and, due to scarcity, are often difficult to properly evaluate for market value.

Split levels must be compared only to other split levels, which is a challenge as there are so many different styles of split levels. Three level and four level splits can be compared, but you must adjust for square footage as only the "above grade" square footage counts in the official size, yet the total usable space is far more than the official size indicates. This makes split levels tricky, especially when you are comparing side splits to back splits. Pay special attention to those which are and are not "walk out" splits. Walk outs are far more attractive to the general market.

Semi-Bungalows, aka, one and a half stories, are usually built before 1967 and usually have a small footprint. These must be only compared to each other, as most buyers either love them or hate them.

Regardless of the style of home, the ceiling height of the basement is a significant factor to consider. In older homes, some basement ceilings are less than the average of 7 foot 8 inches, making them much less desirable, therefore they fetch a lower price than their competition which offers standard height basement ceilings.

In the case of 9 or 10 foot basement ceilings, they are more desirable to many buyers but they only have a minimal resale advantage over basement ceilings of the standard 7 foot 8 inches, which are often inaccurately referred to as 8 foot ceilings.

*****NOTE*****

Square footage is calculated differently under different governing bodies. In Alberta, only square footage which is "above grade" counts.

Location, location, location

When deciding which comparables have a similarly desirable location, you must identify both your **micro and your macro** location variables.

Some **micro** location variables are:

- Inside or outside corner lots
- Through road or secondary through road
- Condition of your neighbour's homes / yards
- Is there alley access?
- If in a crescent, are you at the apex?
- Proximity to the nearest green spaces

Some **Macro** location variables are:

- Desirability of your town
- Desirability of your neighbourhood
- Commuter access to main thoroughfares
- Air pollution

- Noise pollution
- Flood zones
- Proximity to amenities
- Proximity to schools
- Current and future development

Be open to criticism

Reducing your bias when pricing your home is extremely difficult, regardless of who you are or what you do for a living. Below is an excerpt from the book *Why Not Me?*

It takes a big person to accept criticism. Often, people are not able to distinguish between constructive and destructive criticism. Consequently, all they hear when they are criticized is an attack on their character. Constructive criticism comes from a person who cares about you, and this person hopes to help you by shedding a light on what they perceive to be a shortcoming. This criticism is coming from a positive stance and is intended to deliver a positive message. By accepting this information, you are respecting their opinion while not necessarily agreeing with it. By realizing that you are not being attacked, you will be able to remain objective in your decision to agree or disagree with the criticism.

Destructive criticism contains a negative message and comes from a person who is trying to tear you down. If they are trying to tear you down, it isn't necessarily because they don't care about you. When one feels a need to attack, it's usually because they are insecure and feel a need to be superior to you. As with constructive criticism, there is no need to fight back. Just give their opinion the level of respect it deserves and decide to agree or disagree with the criticism. Just because they are coming from a negative stance, it doesn't mean there isn't any merit in what is being said. We shouldn't shy away from opinions that challenge us. None of us is perfect; therefore, we all should be open to criticism. Criticism is a gift that gives you an opportunity to grow.

When in doubt, hire a professional appraiser

I'm not bashing Realtors... I am one. The potential issue with our market evaluations is they may be biased for a number of different reasons. Perhaps the Realtor has ascertained you need to hear a number which is higher than what is realistic so he twists the numbers to make them show what you want to see.

Or, you and your Realtor may strongly disagree with what the proper asking price should be, which is a bad way to start off a business relationship.

Or, maybe you just don't trust your Realtor's judgement and want to be extra certain of having the correct listing price.

A CMA, or "Comparative Market Analysis" tends to be as much an art as it is a science. If you have a really good

Realtor, a CMA can often be more accurate than an appraisal because CMAs consider factors which an appraisal cannot. This is because an appraisal is a legal document which can be used in the court of law, and a CMA is a professional estimate.

A good CMA takes into account the aesthetics of your home and how the current market is likely to respond to it. Also, market pressure, market trends, lending rules, banking climate, economic climate, and neighbourhood reputation are a few of the factors which are considered by a CMA but not by an appraisal. The two should be close but are not always the same. Appraisals tend to be a little lower, depending on the reason the appraisal was done.

Appraisals are done by licensed professionals, but even THEY are subject to bias, depending on who their client is and the current disposition of the client.

Typically, appraisers work directly for the banks. If the bank is in a lending mood, the appraisals are more generous. If the bank is highly cautious, the appraisals tend to be cautious as well. The relationship between appraisals and the bank... is why you NEED to get an appraisal if you don't trust your Realtor.

The bank will insist on appraisals for any conventional mortgage. Appraisals are legal instruments that are not subject to anything but supported facts and are accepted in the court of law. If the property does not appraise at or very near the amount of the offer, the bank will not provide financing and the deal will collapse. If the deal collapses, your house doesn't sell.

CMHC or Genworth mortgages (insured mortgages) don't usually have full appraisals, but they still use internal evaluation systems. These systems are ballpark, but the evaluation still needs to be close or the deal will collapse. Review your most recent tax assessment as it often calculates about 5% higher than what the bank will assess your property at. Both municipal assessments and bank assessments are ballpark but still critical when lenders decide the amount which they are willing to loan.

Either way, if your selling price isn't close, the deal will NOT be funded by the bank.
This leaves you with cash buyers, who are few and far between. They do exist, but they are often very savvy buyers who tend to prey on desperate sellers, and they only tend to pay rock bottom prices.

The bottom line is, financed buyers CAN'T buy because the bank won't fund them, and cash buyers won't buy because they never pay top dollar.

Another difference which you need to factor is an assessment of the appropriate ASKING price, not just a suggested SELLING price. When looking at a CMA, you have to ask the same question... is this what it will SELL for or what I should list it at? Deciding the correct asking price depends on a great deal of factors, and there isn't a good rule of thumb to follow other than... DON'T ASK TOO MUCH! If you are too ambitious, you'll end up with a house that will not sell.

"Can't I just reduce the price later if I don't get lucky?" This is a dangerous game to play. The result of this strategy is usually that your listing becomes tainted as "stale", and is likely to take three times as long to sell, if it sells at all. When or if it does sell, you may receive LESS money than you would have if you had priced it right the first time due to the "stale" stigma.

If you're planning on selling your home by yourself or using a FSBO company, the appraisal is more important than ever. Invest the money and do the job right the first time or you'll risk losing out on your selling price.

Price search parameters

Many search platforms have a drop-down list when people input their search criteria. Even if they don't, people tend to search in fifty thousand dollar price blocks, which is important to remember when you are choosing your price.

For instance, if you feel your home should sell for $490,000.00, but you price your home at $509,999.00 "just in case you get lucky", your home will be invisible to everyone who is looking under $500,000.00.

Not only will you be invisible but you will also be competing with homes of greater value, which means your home will look to be the LEAST attractive of the bunch, as it is not a direct comparison.

Interpreting your tax assessment

Instead of concluding with "the bottom line", I'm going to start with it, and explain why after. The bottom line is:

DO NOT PRICE YOUR HOME BASED SOLELY ON YOUR TAX ASSESSMENT

There are three major ways to assess the value of your home, all each with its own specific purpose:

1. Property tax assessments

This is a **ballpark** estimate of the value of your home in order for your municipality to decide how much property tax to charge you. These assessments are done by an assessor driving past your home or simply checking it out on Google Earth, then making a best guess of what your home is likely worth assuming the interior is in average condition. The assessor also uses MLS data in a broad manner.

2. Market Evaluations

Proper market evaluations are done by a Licensed Realtor who has physically been in your home. The Realtor must have enough experience to understand all of the underlying factors which are outlined in this book. The purpose of a market evaluation is to determine both a **realistic selling price**, as well as a **strategic asking price**.

3. Appraisals

Appraisals are often confused with market evaluations, and although they are similar, they are not the same. Market evaluations are as much an art as they are a science, where **appraisals are all science, and not an art.**

Appraisals are usually done on the behest of the banks or the court system. They are legal documents which are derived from both MLS data and a detailed physical inspection of your home by specialists who are Licensed Appraisers. The appraised price should be similar to the value found by a market evaluation, but they do not always draw the same conclusions as the numbers are based on a different set of criteria, and with a different motivation.

An appraisal has roughly ten times the effort and supporting data than a property tax assessment.

Is your property tax bill too high?

Property taxes are directly proportionate to the value put on your home VIA the municipalities' assessment. The formula includes something called a MIL RATE. The Mil Rate is the number which is increased when the politicians decide to raise your taxes.

There is one OTHER way to increase your taxes which is both stealthy and unethical. If you have a dishonest town council who hires a dishonest tax assessor, there is nothing stopping them from colluding to assess your property at an unrealistically high value.

*****Disclaimer*****

Neither the author nor any of the contributing authors are accusing any particular municipality of this practice. The above scenario of malfeasance is a theory of the author, Mark Meincke, which is based on his personal observations and some alleged precedents.

Interesting note: If you google "property tax scandal", you will find a 2016 article where the Premier of New Brunswick promises to investigate a sudden and significant property tax hike.

Though not commonly covered in the news, I have personally observed several instances where property taxes were increased based on increased property tax assessment values, yet the market evaluations showed no increase in the general market values. The instances which I have observed were never officially investigated as far as I am aware; however, I do find them to be suspicious.

Contesting your property tax assessment

You may be able to contest your property tax assessment, but you cannot procrastinate if you decide to fight your tax bill. In many cases, you **only have two months** after the release of the property assessments to contest the amount your home is valued at. Some municipalities will not accept a Realtor's market evaluation, they will only accept an appraisal from a licensed Appraiser.

There have been instances where people have filed **"class action lawsuits"** against their municipal government as a result of sweeping tax hikes which appeared to be a result of dishonest property tax assessments of property values. Again, a quick search will reveal several cases which occurred in New Brunswick since 2005. Lawsuits should be left as a method of last resort as they are expensive and time consuming. Most municipalities are honest and fair when reviewing your assessment appeal.

In one extreme example of which I was personally involved in, a potential client wanted to list their home for sale with me so they asked for a full market evaluation. When I presented my evaluation to them, they were shocked by the low number of $850,000.00. They were even more surprised to realize that upon my explanation of how I arrived at that number, they actually agreed with my assessment of value. I found out later that I was the third Realtor which they had asked, and the other two evaluations were similar in conclusion to mine.

My client's shock and disappointment was based on the home value which was assessed by the City. According to the City, their home was worth $1,250,000.00, and they were being taxed accordingly. They were disappointed to find out their home was not worth as much as they had hoped, and they were justifiably angry to find out they had been paying significantly more in property tax than what was fair.

Section Notes

What was my greatest take-away from this section?

What do I need to remember about this section?

8

How Much Should I Offer When I'm Buying?

The short answer for most situations is "Fair Market Value". Based on all of the above factors to consider when pricing a property, I usually encourage buyers to make an offer just below what you feel is a fair selling price, leaving enough room to negotiate back and forth if necessary. A crude but appropriate old saying about being greedy is, "Pigs get slaughtered". The people who are always looking to take advantage of others often end up further behind, not further ahead. This being said, every seller is different, and the amount of negotiation room you factor in will be based on the information you are able to glean from the seller and the seller's agent if they are represented. If they are the wheeler-dealer type, you will have to factor in a larger spread for wiggle room. If they are straight shooters, you would factor in far less room for the negotiation process.

An exception to this advice might be for some professional Real Estate investors. One person I know who has over 250 properties will usually make 8-12 offers for each accepted offer. He only jumps on the deals where there are desperate sellers who are forced to sell for less than fair market value. I don't condemn this practice, but it's not one I promote either. For you to get a "great deal", someone else will get ripped off. The person being ripped off usually needs the money more than you do, so keep this in mind when deciding on your negotiation strategy.

Also, if you use this tactic when buying a home, you will always be compromising on the home because you're focused on the best deal, not the best home for you and your family.

The first offer is the best offer

With the exception of multiple-offer situations, most Realtors will advise a seller to give strong consideration to the first offer which is received. Most often, any subsequent offers will end up netting the seller less than the original offer which was refused. In practice, I've seen this play out time and time again, leaving the seller with a "woulda, coulda, shoulda" scenario. Being greedy often results in receiving a lower than possible selling price.

On the other side, if you are making an offer on a property and the seller has refused offers in the past, you might be in a position of opportunity. Just because a seller has refused a previous offer does not mean they are not regretting their decision. Also, as time passes, some sellers get more and more desperate to sell.

The early bird gets the deal

The best deal I ever put together for a client was written at full list price. The property had been on the market for 27 days and no offers had yet come in. When we viewed the property, it was clear to me and the buyers that the home was under-priced by over $100,000.00. When we decided to write the offer, we didn't want to leave anything to chance. My clients wrote the offer at full list price and removed their conditions eight days later. With the stroke of a pen, my clients made an instant profit of $100,000.00. Had they decided to push their luck by offering a lower price, the door would have been open for others to swoop in and outbid us.

The bottom line is, when you find a great house at a great price, don't look the gift horse in the mouth. Pull out your pen and get the offer signed as fast as possible before some other bargain hunter closes the deal.

What will it cost you for required renovations?

It's easy to fall in love with a home. Once you do, it's also easy to start discounting any renovations that may be required. Recently, I was showing acreage, and the house was fantastic. The views were great and the location was convenient. However, the septic system was at the end of its life span, with a replacement cost of about $40,000.000. Also, they needed to build a shop, with a cost of another $40,000.00. When factoring in the added $80,000.00 required to get the home functional for them, the asking price was far too high. For a different family, the asking price may have been reasonable, as a shop would not be required. Also, if someone owned a back-hoe and could build their own septic system, the price would have been fantastic.

When offering a price, there is more to it than just factoring market value; you have to also factor what the home is worth to you in your individual situation. A home might be priced well for someone else, but priced wrong for you.

Market potential

How much you offer should also depend on how much ROI (Return On Investment) potential the property has. For instance, if the home looks great but has old windows, ancient mechanical, and a 25 year old roof, the price better reflect getting all three of those items up-to-date.

Conversely, if a home has new windows, mechanical and roof but really needs flooring and paint, you may be looking at an ideal revenue property. The remaining renovations in this case all have the potential to yield a high ROI. The more ROI potential a property has, the higher the potential net profit post-renovations.

Section Notes

What was my greatest take-away from this section?

What do I need to remember about this section?

9

You Can Skip Breakfast, But Do NOT Skip a Home Inspection

I've attended dozens of home inspections over the years, and I learn something new almost every time. One glaring observation I've made is how home inspections are often misunderstood and undervalued by the layperson.

A home inspection is NOT:

- A test which is to be passed or failed
- Verification of building code compliance
- Public information; only the person who pays for the inspection has the right to view or share the information
- Intended as a tool to re-negotiate the agreed selling price
- A "to-do" list the sellers must complete prior to possession

- Just for pre-owned homes
- Performed by anyone but a Licensed Home Inspector (unless mutually agreed upon to allow an unlicensed person to perform the inspection)
- A warranty or guarantee of the condition of the home (with some limited exceptions)
- Intended to provide you with a contractor's quote for the cost of repairs
- Invasive; a home inspector cannot damage the home in order to check behind walls or under floors, though some home inspectors do have infrared equipment which can check for continuity of insulation or for the presence of moisture
- Required by the banks for financing
- Part of the appraisal process
- 100% dependable, as there are numerous factors that may prevent a home inspector from discovering or detecting various issues at the time of the inspection, e.g.: snow cover may conceal grading issues

A home inspection IS:

- A non-invasive, visual inspection of all the different systems of your home to ascertain the condition of each individual system
- Sometimes an unofficial verification that your appliances are operational at the time of inspection
- An optional to-do list for the buyer to be aware of

- A search for any significant or costly repairs which may be required but are not expected by the buyer
- A valuable tool to ensure the physical safety of the buyer (I have been at inspections where unexpected and potentially lethal physical threats were found)
- Just as important (maybe more so) for **new homes** as for pre-owned homes
- Potentially a sales feature, e.g.: when the homeowner pays for a pre-home inspection which is offered to potential buyers at no cost
- An important tool to provide peace of mind to the buyer
- Intended to discover past problems and predict future issues such as, but not limited to: flooding, fire, mould and asbestos

Expert Insight from Robyn Ross

To expand a little on what a home inspection is not, I'd like to add that building codes are constantly evolving. For instance, a home that was built to code in 1950 could not possibly be expected to pass current code requirements.

Another way to think of a home inspection is as a "snapshot" in time of the home and its components on that particular day. Those conditions may change the very next day, which in turn change the condition of the home.

For instance, I could inspect a home on March 2nd with two feet of snow on the ground. On March 3rd, all the snow could melt and the basement could flood, drastically changing the condition of the home.

Why use a home inspector at all?

Many know of a "handy uncle" or someone along those lines who they feel could do the job sufficiently. Other than the lack of specific training, your "Handy Uncle Andy" won't likely have a list of satisfied inspection clients who can confirm the perceived quality of Handy Andy's inspections. This has the homeowner crossing their fingers and hoping for the best.

Gambling on your home inspection is a pretty big gamble, and I'd give 4-1 odds that critical items will be missed due to both the lack of specific training and the lack of proper specialty tools for the job (E.g.: moisture meter, infrared camera, infrared thermometer, multi-system checklist).

Whomever you use, make sure they are registered with the jurisdiction of authority, licensed and insured. In Alberta, Canada, where I practice, it is the law that you need to be registered / licensed by the province, and you also need to provide proof of insurance.

Why would I need to get a brand new home inspected?

As a professional tradesman with many years of experience, I can tell you that not all contractors are created equal. What one homebuilder deems acceptable trade practice, another may regard as inferior workmanship or a deficiency. It really depends on who the contractor is looking out for. Oftentimes it's themselves as opposed to the prospective homebuyers.

I once performed a home inspection on a brand new, "ready to move into" home, and one item I flagged was a long, ridged crack in the basement concrete floor extending from one wall to the next. The homebuilder downplayed the possible severity of the problem and said it was nothing to worry about. Conversely, I have been involved in projects with other builders where if that problem appeared, it would have been deemed a deficiency by their Quality Control (QC) team and rectified before it went on the market or handed over to the new owners.

The first homebuilder may have estimated the cost to repair the crack as too great and decided to risk having the new owners accept it as it was versus performing the expensive repair.

When it comes to selecting a builder, it's best to have a list of possible builders and do your research on each one, paying particular attention to customer satisfaction, company stability and build quality. New homes are often a riskier purchase in certain ways than a pre-owned home simply because a new home hasn't had time for the issues to show up.

Think of a home as a human being. When we are young, say up to 30 years old, we are like a new home. We are both looking and feeling good, with few medical problems. It's not until we are 30-50 years old where congenital problems start showing up, like heart disease, etc. A home is much the same; it's not until it's been around for a few years that problems may show up.

Back to the human analogy, if people take care of themselves, e.g. eat well, exercise and live a clean life, it increases their odds of being healthy as they age. If a house and all its components are regularly maintained, the odds of it being a good purchase to another buyer is increased; however, if no maintenance is done, it may need major repairs sooner than it would otherwise.

Both the best and the worst things that can happen to a home are a result of "the homeowners"

There are many homeowners who consider themselves "handy". While some basic home maintenance items such as painting can be effectively (but not professionally) performed by an average homeowner, the majority of projects are best left to the professionals.

There is a barrage of home improvement shows on television, and how-to videos online, which can make many renovations look more simple than they actually are. Often, handy homeowners undertake maintenance or renovation projects which are more difficult than they bargained for.

The resultant work may be unsafe, substandard, in violation of codes, or just plain ugly.

Home maintenance

Most homeowners are unaware of, or just haven't thought about the fact that there is a maximum usable lifespan to almost every component of a home. The neglect of one item will affect the lifespan of another item, which may affect the next, etc.

For example: A typical home with wood trim around the windows has joints in between the pieces of trim which have to be caulked in order to prevent moisture from getting into the trim. Caulking has an average lifespan of five to ten years. Once it is past its serviceable life, the caulking needs to be stripped and reapplied. If this doesn't occur, moisture will get into the trim, wooden window frames and inside the walls. The wood will rot and mould may grow. This is just one of the preventative measures many homeowners neglect, which results in significant damage being done to the home.

Pro tip: Follow a homeowner's maintenance schedule

Utilizing reputable professional contractors to undertake the work provides the safest way for homeowners to renovate and provides the best results in workmanship. This will ensure that all components of the home will last as long as possible and keep the home in tip-top condition.

Renovations / development

Projects such as these should never be undertaken by the unqualified. Appropriate building permits should be taken out and copies need to be made available. Professional tradesmen should always be involved to perform the work, even if it's just to consult. A professional tradesman should be well versed on current building codes, be up-to-date on the latest installation products and methods, and is the most likely to deliver a quality result.

Pro Tip: Check for references

Once Upon a Time…

I was inspecting a home built in the mid-1980s. The main level was in good condition, seemingly well-constructed and decently maintained. All was looking good until I went into the D.I.Y. developed basement. The ceilings were drywall and the center of each 4x8 drywall sheet was sagging down quite noticeably. The basement development was done by the previous homeowner without any building permits. He had only fastened the sheets of drywall on the edges, and failed to fasten the middle of the sheets. After a short period of time, gravity did what it does and the sheets sagged. **The entire ceiling needed to be ripped down and reinstalled by a qualified tradesman.**

The poor quality of the ceiling cast serious doubt on the quality of the framing, insulation, vapour barrier, and electrical, which was hidden behind the drywall of the D.I.Y. partition and parameter walls. The only way to be sure it was done right was to rip down all the existing drywall on the walls as well as the ceiling.

Pro Tip: Beware of new paint

When looking at a prospective home, be cognisant of areas of new paint or wall repairs. There are a few reasons why a homeowner will spend the money on a fresh coat of paint prior to listing.

The obvious reason is to increase its odds of selling / increasing value. This is what most people's perceptions would be. However, there can be nefarious reasons as well, such as covering undisclosed damage. If, while looking at the home, you notice one wall has been recently painted and there are signs of a drywall repair, you have to question why.

I looked at a home once where the bay window trim had been painted just before being listed. At first glance everything appeared to be on the up and up and it seemed to be just regular maintenance being performed. Upon a closer look with my moisture meter, it was found that **the bottom of the wooden bay window frame was rotten**. A strip of trim was added, caulked, and a heavy coat of paint applied over it to cover the rotten part.

"Splash and dash"

There would most likely have been further damage to the inside of the wall as well. Homeowners who keep a regular home maintenance schedule and use qualified specialists can expect to get the maximum revenue when they sell their house with the fewest defects found by the home inspector. Homeowners who are unaware that regular maintenance is required and/or uses unqualified people to do what is done can expect many defects on an inspection report, and this can affect the final selling price or ease by which the home is sold.

Pre-sale home inspections

Having your home inspected prior to listing it is a growing trend. The prospective seller must realize that the inspector is obligated to give an honest and unbiased report, regardless of who is paying for his services. If the home is in good condition and no major items are flagged, then having the inspection report to offer can streamline the sale process and maximize revenue. If the home is in disrepair and the inspection report indicates defects, the seller may be creating more work for himself as he may want to repair the defects prior to listing the home. Conversely, he may choose not to remediate the deficiencies and have the listing price reflect this fact.

Important to note: If you have your home inspected and it brings to light repairs that need to be made, you are obligated to disclose the issue

and you are also not allowed to modify the inspection report unless done so by the inspector after he confirms the repairs have been done.

ASBESTOS!!!

This is a scary word to lots of people. Asbestos was widely used in construction of homes until 1980 in products such as plaster, ceiling textures, floor tiles and pipe insulation to name a few. The truth is, asbestos is only **dangerous if it's disturbed** and its particles become airborne. Once airborne, even a single inhaled strand increases the risk of major health problems like lung cancer and asbestosis.

If asbestos is encapsulated or sealed with a product that prevents it from becoming airborne, the risks are minimal. If the intent of a homebuyer is to renovate an older home, this would obviously disturb the asbestos and send it into the air.

It is very difficult to positively identify if something contains asbestos. The only way to be 100% sure is to have an asbestos inspection performed where samples are collected by a professional testing company and sent to a lab for identification. Such an inspection could be a very valuable tool when selling a home in this era. Some home inspectors are trained and certified to be able to offer this service as well.

Septic fields / mounds

If you are the owner of a property that utilizes a private septic system as opposed to a public system, you have some work to do to keep it working properly.

Best practises include:

- Not parking equipment or storing anything on top of the field
- Having the tank cleaned in keeping with the manufacturers' recommendations
- Having it inspected by a professional septic system company
- Keeping records of regular maintenance of the septic system
- Ensuring the tank lids are on correctly and in good condition
- Maintaining and replacing the septic pump per your maintenance schedule

Section Notes

What was my greatest take-away from this section?

What do I need to remember about this section?

10

Legal Land Mines - "Let Him Beware"

by James C. Lozinsky

This addresses information with respect to buying and selling used residential homes. This section does not cover the multitude of other concerns that may arise from other types of real estate transactions such as new homes, acreage, bare land, construction contracts, farm or agricultural property, rental property, and commercial or mixed use property, although a lot of the concepts and information are applicable to other situations.

Caveats, writs & liens... oh my!

Caveats, writs and liens are terms often confused with each other, and their separate functions are rarely understood. More importantly is the potential impact these legal instruments have on the purchaser of a property which must be clearly understood.

Let's start with the basic definitions:

Caveat: Caveat is Latin for "let him beware". You may have heard the Latin terms *caveat emptor*, which means "let the buyer beware" and *caveat lector*, which means "let the reader beware". In its simplest definition, a caveat is notice of an interest in land. caveats are the most powerful of the three instruments because they are placed on titles to protect third parties who are claiming a registered interest in the property. The caveat may or may not be valid, but you need to determine its validity and how to deal with it prior to committing to buying or selling that property.

Writ: Writ is the second most powerful legal instrument and is also placed on the property title. A writ is a legal instrument granted by the court in order to secure a debt which is not directly related to the subject property. There are different methods to remedy a writ registered against a title, and the best method is determined by the circumstances.

Lien: There are different types of liens, but the most common is the **"Builder's Lien".** This is placed when construction services are performed on the property, and the owner is withholding some or all of the money owed to the contractor. The lien must be replaced by a claim in court if it is not satisfied within a certain time limit.

One of the concerns a buyer should have regarding these legal instruments is whether the seller has sufficient funds to pay in full to have them discharged. If the seller cannot discharge these from title, they will not be able to convey title to you and the transaction will not complete. If there are builder's liens or writs on a title, as a buyer you want to make sure no more appear on the title prior to completion day. It is good to get terms written into the contract that puts an onus on the seller and will also address what will happen if something else arises pertaining to title.

As a buyer, you want to ensure that the seller has the legal right and ability to sell the property and convey clear title to you. Clear title means that when you take over the property the seller has paid or will pay them on closing, and all caveats / writs / liens will be discharged from the title. The real estate lawyer you use to look after your interests will ensure that these are paid and discharged, but it should be determined as early as possible whether there are sufficient funds to provide a clear title.

Easements, Encroachments, Relaxations, Restrictive Covenants and what to do about them

Easement: An Easement allows an owner of land to use land owned by another party in some way. There are conditions that need to be met in order for the easement to be validly registered on a title. Some common purposes of an easement are: to allow access to and from property, drainage, parking, and maintaining and servicing utilities.

Encroachments: An Encroachment grants an exclusive or unrestricted use of the land to another owner of land. Usually an encroachment arises from the building of a structure or improvement that extends past the property line and onto the neighbouring lot.

Relaxations: A Relaxation occurs when a structure is built on one parcel of land but it is built too close to the boundary or too close to a right of way. The municipality may choose to allow a relaxation by way of an application to allow the structure to remain. If the municipality does not allow a relaxation, the structure has to be altered, relocated within the boundaries or completely removed.

Restrictive Covenants: Restrictive Covenants (RCs) exist to control the use and development of the land. There are certain requirements that have to be met to make an RC enforceable.

You are deemed to be aware of and understand any documents which are registered on a title. The registration of the above items on a title is giving public notice that they are on the title. A prudent buyer or seller will review the title and any documents with their lawyer so they understand and know how it affects the property, as well as how it may affect their future plans for the property.

There are ways to have any of the above documents removed from a title, as some documents are more complex than others and may involve court applications and court orders. The simplest to have something removed from a title are the financial ones. Those have to be paid out in full by the seller then discharged so the buyer gets the property with a clear title.

If you want to remove a non-financial registration from a title, you should make sure you understand what it does and why you want it removed because removing it affects not only your property and your rights, but the rights and obligations of the surrounding lots to your property.

Title insurance

Title insurance gained popularity between 2004 and 2010; however, since roughly 2014, most lawyers rarely recommend it. The role of title insurance is to protect the buyer, and may also protect the lender, if a defect is discovered in the future. The defect can be title-related or non-title related. Title insurance is a no-fault basis, meaning it does not matter who is at fault. If a defect is discovered, the insurer either pays to fix the problem or fixes the problem.

The original goal of title insurance was to allow quicker closings of real estate transactions so the buyer would not have to pay late interest while waiting for registration of land titles. This is called gap coverage which covers the gap between possession and mortgage funds being released.

This was common when the land title office was three to six weeks behind in registrations.

Title insurance can cover items such as future title fraud and gap coverage, as stated above, where there is a delay in registration of the transfer, no Real Property Report (RPR), deficiencies that do not show up on the Real Property Report (RPR), deficiencies that are hidden and not on an RPR, and it may even cover known deficiencies that are on the RPR under certain circumstances.

However, title insurance can be problematic because it does not reveal any property issues that may exist; it is simply an insurance policy that covers any issues that the buyer may later discover. Another concern arises when a buyer buys without an RPR and accepts title insurance in lieu of an RPR with compliance. When that buyer wants to sell, he will likely need an RPR with compliance to sell, and he will incur that cost, as well as the cost and delays of remedying any issues the RPR may reveal.

RPRs with compliance

An RPR (Real Property Report) is a legal document which is an official survey of the property. An RPR can be any age, as long it is accurate and has a stamp of compliance from the municipality. Some lenders demand an RPR that is not beyond a number of years in age, regardless of whether it has compliance.

In addition to being accurate, an RPR must have the **stamp from your municipality** showing it is **"compliant"** with regulations of your particular municipality. An RPR shows the measurements of the lot and buildings, the distances between buildings, and the distances between buildings and property lines, right of ways, etc. Also on an RPR, you'll find utility right of ways, drainage swales and encroachments. It is important to have an accurate RPR with compliance prior to listing your home, as it may cause delays and holdbacks on closing if the RPR has not been provided to the buyer to review in advance.

When there is a utility right of way on your RPR, this means your municipality has the right to access the right of way and perform any required work within the boundary of that right away. This includes installing power boxes or digging trenches for the purpose of accessing utilities. When this happens, the municipality is required to tidy up after and repair any damage they've caused to you, your yard or fence, etc.

What is on a title?

Before you sell, and especially before you buy a property, it is imperative that you view a current copy of the title and see what is registered on that title. If you buy without looking at the title, you are deemed to have known what was registered on the title regardless, and you have to live with it. As a seller, you want to make sure your title is clean to ensure there are no surprises on closing day that cause delays or cost you money in order to discharge to complete the sale.

Property tax, condo fees, resident association fees – adjustments on closing

Property taxes are calculated on a calendar year basis, from January 1 to December 31 of each year. However, the invoice for property taxes is not issued by the municipality until about halfway through the year. Each municipality is different, but the tax invoice is usually issued sometime between June and September. The seller is liable for the taxes until the completion day, and the buyer is liable for the taxes after closing date. The real estate lawyers working on the file will make adjustments to the purchase price that will apportion between the seller and the buyer their respective liability for the taxes paid to the municipality.

Condo fees are calculated and paid monthly. These are adjusted by the lawyers on a monthly basis. Resident association fees can be a monthly or a yearly fee and are also adjusted and apportioned on completion day.

Proper possession dates

Regardless of whether you are writing the offer or accepting an **offer to purchase**, make sure the completion day is never ever on a weekend, a Friday, or a Thursday which precedes a Friday holiday or a statutory holiday. Why, you may ask? The short answer is because "stuff happens". Every so often there's a delay in one part of the process that prevents the possession from happening on time. If the delay is an entire day and that day happens to be followed by either a weekend or holiday, you'll have to wait until the following regular business day in order to close the deal.

The result is either possession is delayed or you pay late interest to the seller under a tenancy at will agreement. You get possession, but you cannot do anything with the property until the transaction has completed. Either way, it creates issues, potentially increases costs and causes last minute changes. It is best to be avoided if possible.

Make sure the house you bought is the house you receive

If you get the feeling that the current owners might not leave the home in the same or better condition than it was when you decided to purchase it, you may wish to include in the contract a **"Holdback".** A Holdback is an amount of money that the buyer holds back from the seller until the condition of the holdback is verified on possession date.

The purpose of holdbacks is to compensate the buyer for their time and costs for such things as:

- Abandoned belongings left behind that have to be hauled away

- If the home is filthy
- There is damage discovered on possession day
- If the seller removed items which were supposed to stay in the house

There are different ways to write a holdback into an offer, and a Realtor and real estate lawyer know how to word the holdback for each situation so you are properly protected by the contract. The fair way to deal with a holdback, if it arises, is to only use the money you require and refund the balance to the sellers.

Mutual pros – Holdbacks deal with potential issues before they happen, with an agreement to plan to resolve them or to compensate the party who has suffered. If the holdback is worded properly, it will help avoid costly litigation and delays because they set out each party's rights in advance.

Buyer's cons – A holdback may "muddy the waters" of the deal, as the seller may be reluctant to agree to any holdbacks in advance, thereby reducing the buyer's negotiation power.

Seller's cons– A holdback has the potential of being abused by withholding it based on unreasonable or unsubstantiated grounds. In this circumstance, the only option may be to fight in court, which is likely to incur significant costs.

You know what happens when you assume, right? Re: Assumption of mortgage

A mortgage assumption may be attractive to a seller if the seller has trouble finding a buyer and wants to sell the property sooner rather than waiting or if the seller wants to avoid paying mortgage payout penalties. An assumption may be attractive to a buyer when interest rates are rising and the current mortgage is locked in at a low interest rate.

Some believe that all mortgages are assumable, but this is not entirely correct. The buyer trying to assume the mortgage has to be qualified by the lender to assume the mortgage. The seller and buyer cannot agree on their own that the buyers will assume the mortgage.

Another common misconception about assuming mortgages is that the seller is off the hook once the buyer assumes the mortgage. Even when the buyer assumes the mortgage with lender approval, the original mortgage holder is still potentially liable for the payments for the life of the mortgage and through all future renewals. The seller is only off the hook once the person who assumed the mortgage pays it out either by sale or by refinancing with a new mortgage. There are circumstances where the lender agrees to release the seller from all liability but certain circumstances have to be met for that to occur.

The bottom line is that a seller should not let a buyer assume their mortgage because if the buyer does not meet the payments or other terms of the mortgage, the lender may foreclose on the house and the seller may still be liable for any shortfall.

Rent-to own risks

A seller or a buyer may think a rent-to-own situation will give them relief from the financial demands they are experiencing or they may have other reasons for considering a rent-to-own arrangement, such as the seller may be having trouble finding a buyer at his asking price or soon enough to relieve him of the financial burden of paying the costs of carrying the property.

A buyer may want to buy but does not yet have the deposit money needed to make a purchase outright or the right credit rating to qualify for a mortgage. The seller's risk in taking on a rent-to-own is that the seller may enter the transaction with a buyer that causes damages to the property and/or is consistently late with payments or misses payments. This further delays the seller's ability to sell the property and adds extra costs to evict the buyer and perform necessary repairs. **On the buyer's side, if the buyer never acquires the financial means to complete the purchase, he would lose the deposit and all monies paid are forfeited to the seller.** It is very important that the wording in the rent-to-own contract covers and protects both parties and sets out their rights clearly, not only with respect to each other but also with respect to the property.

Seller's liability re: latent and patent defects

A latent defect is a defect which cannot be discovered by using normal means to inspect the property. If it is a latent defect and the defect has significant consequences for the buyer or the defect materially changes the house that the buyer contracted to buy, the seller may be liable for damages. The latent defect would be one that had the buyer known of the defect, they would not have purchased it or they would have paid substantially less for the property. In this situation, the seller may then be liable to the buyer for not disclosing the defect prior to the contract being entered into or for not honestly answering questions about the property and disclosing the latent defect.

Patent defects are problems with the property that the buyer could have or should have discovered had they performed a thorough inspection. It is buyer beware. The buyer has to ensure that they have done all they can to inspect the house and property to find any defects. A patent defect may be something such as a broken handrail a hole in the wall or a stain on the floor. These are defects that the buyer should be able to easily see upon inspection of the home. A seller does not have to reveal patent defects; it is up to the buyer to discover them. The buyer should do everything they can to discover all patent defects.

There are a number of steps the buyer can take to protect themselves against defects of any kind. One is to hire a certified and thorough property inspector, another is to review a year or two of utility bills to see usage and to ask the seller specific questions.

Seller / Vendor financing: do's and don'ts

Sometimes a buyer may not be able to meet all the lender's conditions to qualify for a mortgage. A seller may want to finance the buyer to buy the property by giving the buyer a mortgage or what is also called a Vendor Take-Back mortgage (VTB). To ensure that your take-back mortgage and seller financing are complete with as much protection for the seller as possible, you should use a lawyer to prepare the documents.

A take-back mortgage is only possible if the seller has no existing mortgage on the property or already has the funds to pay-out the seller's current mortgage. The seller cannot transfer title to the buyer and leave his current mortgage unpaid because of the terms of his mortgage. With a VTM, the buyer has no funds to give to the seller to pay out the seller's mortgage because the buyer is not using a lender to receive funds from. The first potential problem for the seller is that the seller will not receive the full purchase price as a lump sum and will not have any money to pay off his existing mortgage or to invest elsewhere, or to use for other purposes.

A second problem is that the seller is then the lender and he / she has to be prepared to foreclose on the property if it becomes necessary to do so. Banks and other big lenders are set up to enforce foreclosures and they have the financial resources and the team to do so. A seller who has to foreclose on a take-back mortgage has to spend time and money to enforce the mortgage and, if necessary, to foreclose and evict the buyer. This involves a series of court applications which take time, and as time goes by, the seller is not receiving any payments from the buyer and is spending money to foreclose on the buyer.

"Subject to lawyer's approval"

Sometimes when people are selling their home without a Realtor's representation, they place "subject to lawyer's approval" as a condition in the purchase contract. This is a wise condition to have; however, it must be understood that construction of a purchase contract that suits your individual situation is not the primary expertise of a real estate lawyer.

The expertise of a real estate lawyer is enforcement of the terms of the purchase contract, not the negotiation of it. A lawyer will be able to advise you on how the terms of the contract affect you and what options you have with respect to those terms, but a lawyer is not there to help you negotiate those terms in relation to agreeing to a contract.

Realtors are experts when it comes to knowing how to best customize the conditions and terms of the purchase contract, and to negotiate them in a manner that not only protects you from liability but also ensures that you maintain the **best possible negotiation position**.

Realtors are often in a position to be privy to information that your lawyer is not; such as the reputation and disposition of the opposing Realtor, measuring market pressure, and ascertaining the seller's or buyer's motivation.

Another example is predicting which chattels may be contentious issues and how to mitigate the issues before they happen. The Realtor sees and visits the house with you, and discusses the house with you as you go through it.

Attached and unattached goods

When writing your contract, both the seller and buyer need to be aware of whether an item is classified as an attached or an unattached good as each of these are treated differently.

E.g.: The rules state that if something is affixed to the home then it is "attached" and therefore not a chattel. It is expected to remain as part of the home.

Note: Water softeners fall into a little known grey area of whether they should be mentioned as an attached or unattached good. On possession day, a buyer may be shocked to discover that the water softener has been removed and they may have no recourse. Water softeners, security systems, and sprinkler systems are examples of items which should be specified in the purchase contract. When in doubt, be sure to specify what is and is not expected to be included with the home on possession day. Hood fans are often itemized on purchase agreements, even though they are always affixed. It is better to be safe than sorry.

For the seller, it is best to itemize any items which you do not intend to include with the home. To avoid putting yourself in legal jeopardy, make sure the purchase contract is very clear on what items you intend to remove from the property, and which items you intend to leave behind.

Deposits

Price deposits and additional deposits are all part of the negotiation process and also fall under the specific expertise of Realtors. Knowing the right way to put all the pieces together requires a front-line knowledge of all the players involved. If you are slack in your negotiation approach, you lose your footing as a negotiator.

Ascertaining the disposition of the seller and understanding how to use that knowledge to your advantage can only be done by a select few Realtors who have the correct training. By viewing a home, a skilled Realtor who is trained in D.I.S.C. can infer the seller's personality type based on the D.I.S.C. analysis of the home. D.I.S.C is a powerful personality profiling tool which, if used correctly, can increase your bargaining position by tailoring your negotiation of the purchase contract accordingly, and by presenting the offer to the seller accordingly. Lessons on the D.I.S.C. are abundantly available on YouTube, although they are not a great replacement for a full and engaging course.

Understanding the difference between "conditions" and "terms" in the contract and how to properly use them

The **condition** is part of a contract that has to be satisfied or waived to make the contract binding and enforceable. It basically says, "I will commit to buy this house **IF**…"

The most common "Ifs" are usually:
IF I get the bank to provide financing on suitable terms
IF I'm happy with the results of the home inspection
IF I can sell my home first
IF I'm happy with my due diligence
IF I'm satisfied after reviewing the previous six months of utility bills
IF my wife also views the house and agrees to buy

Regardless of which **IF** you place as a condition, the contract will set an agreed-upon date by which your **IF** will have to be satisfied or waived, or the contract dies. **Both the buyer and the seller have the ability to include**

conditions of the contract. Once the conditions are all satisfied or waived, you now have a **firm deal**, which is legally binding to both parties.

After conditions are either satisfied or waived, the deposit money is now forfeited at this point should the buyer choose to back out of the contract.

Terms

Contract **terms** are quite different from contract conditions. Terms are the nuts and bolts of the contract which describe what each party is committing to do and when they will complete it by.

Once the conditions are satisfied / waived / removed, **all terms are binding**, so be sure you have read and understand the entire contract carefully. Most purchase contracts are standard templates, so you need to make sure any terms which you cannot meet or you want altered are either struck out or altered accordingly prior to signing the contract.

What is "non-performance" and what are the consequences?

If one party fails to abide by the terms of the contract, they are "non-performing" or in breach of the contract. The most common example of non-performance happens when a buyer can not or will not complete the purchase. This leaves the seller stuck with the property and without the money the seller was counting on receiving. When this occurs, the buyer forfeits all deposits paid and the monies become the property of the seller. In addition to keeping the deposit monies, the seller can also sue the buyer for non-performance of the contract and receive an award of damages that the buyer has to pay to the seller.

If the seller changes their mind and refuses to close, the buyer can sue the seller for specific performance, meaning they are forcing the seller to transfer title to them as per the contract or in lieu of specific performance, the buyer may receive an award of damages.

Choosing a real estate lawyer and understanding their role

If the lawyer you are considering does not regularly handle real estate transactions, you should choose a different lawyer. As with all aspects of law, you are usually best off choosing an experienced specialist who has seen more scenarios than you can possibly imagine.

Real estate transactions can appear to be simple and straightforward from a legal standpoint, but there is a lot under the surface and they are also a fertile breeding ground for the bizarre and unpredictable. When the latter occurs, you want an expert on your side that will be both your advocate and your guide throughout the transaction.

Section Notes

What was my greatest take-away from this section?

What do I need to remember about this section?

11

The Case for the RPR

by Nathan Prins

What is a Real Property Report?

A Real Property Report is a legal document which clearly illustrates the location of significant visible improvements relative to property boundaries. It takes the form of a plan or illustration of the various physical features of the property, including a written statement detailing the surveyor's opinions or concerns. It can be relied upon by the buyer, the seller, the lender and the municipality as an accurate representation of the improvements on a piece of property.

Real Property Reports equip all parties involved:

- Problems identified that can be **resolved** before a sale is finalized

- Sellers **know** accurate locations and dimensions of buildings, improvements, rights-of-way, and encroachments relative to boundaries of their property
- Purchasers **know** the physical dimensions of the property
- Financing usually requires **verified** survey information
- Property transactions are simplified
- Development and building permits **require** boundary information

What title insurance claims

Title insurance is a policy designed to protect the **title owner** against challenges to ownership related to title defects. A defect is a problem with the title that prevents free and clear ownership.

Title insurance is designed to protect against:

- Fraud and forgery, including someone taking your title through fraud or forgery (see the FYI below)
- Encroachments **that would be disclosed** by a new survey
- Easements over the property **that would be disclosed** by a new survey
- Zoning non-compliance
- Someone other than the homeowner having interest (i.e. a previous owner of the property not being discharged from the title)

- The policy can provide broader coverage than a solicitor / notary's opinion on the title as well as **post purchase fraud coverage**
- If there are defects affecting the title that are covered by the title insurance policy, the title insurer **may** take steps to rectify the problem

The problems with title insurance:

- Title insurance may be a worthwhile investment in the United States or other Canadian jurisdictions operating with a deeds title system
- Titles are **guaranteed against Fraud and Forgery** by the Alberta Government (Torrens system)
- Titles in Alberta, British Columbia and Saskatchewan are guaranteed to be an accurate representation of interest in title (there is no need to look further than the title), therefore there is no need for fraud coverage
- If there are defects with ownership (garage over right of way, neighbours fence is incorrectly placed, etc., **<u>title insurance does not fix the problem, it only hides it</u>**
- The steps taken by the title insurer may only fix the violation, not rectify the issue. For example, if a fence or garage is built in the wrong place or over an easement, title insurance may only pay to remove the structure, not erect a new one in the correct place.

Purchasing a property may be the largest financial investment you ever make. With a Real Property report, owners are aware of any boundary problems, issues with municipal compliance, and the extents of rights of way and the property. They will know whether their new home is too close to the property line, part of their garage is on their neighbour's land, or vice versa.

Knowledge is power. Purchasers, sellers, municipalities and real estate professionals are urged to be equipped by knowing and resolving the issues with a property instead of turning a blind eye with a service that offers little value.

FYI

The Torrens system operates under the authority of the Land Titles Act, a provincial law. It states that the Government of Alberta has custody of all original titles, documents and plans, and has the legal responsibility for the validity and security of all registered land titles information. The government guarantees the accuracy of all titles, and in order to do this, operates an Assurance Fund to compensate anyone who suffers a loss due to an error on a title or a fraudulent transaction.

References

[1] Alberta Land Surveyor's Association,http://www.alsa.ab.ca/PublicInformation/RealPropertyReports.aspx

[2] RBC – Title Insurance,http://www.rbcroyalbank.com/mortgages/title-insurance.html

[3] Canadian Legal FAQ's, Centre for Public Legal Education,http://www.law-faqs.org/alberta-faqs/real-estate-and-renting/land-titles/

Section Notes

What was my greatest take-away from this section?

What do I need to remember about this section?

12

What is Mortgage Fraud and How Does it Affect Me?

There are several types of Mortgage fraud to watch out for, and one of the most common types is the use of a **"Straw Buyer"**. Some shady property investors try to exploit CMHC or Genworth (mortgage insurance) by hiring a "first time home buyer" to purchase a property on behalf of the investor. The pitch may sound something like this:

"Hey, would you like to make an easy $5,000.00 just for filling out some paperwork? All you have to do is write an offer on this house and I will provide all the money required to do the deal. I just need you to have the house in your name in the beginning, and to secure the mortgage. Once the house is yours, I'll assume the mortgage from you, fix the place up and sell it. Once it's sold, you are free and clear

with an easy $5,000.00 in your pocket. I assume all the risk and you get free money!"

What the fraudster doesn't tell you is that you are participating in a crime. All the criminal wants is to minimize their down payment by exploiting either "first time home buyer" rules or CMHC options. Also, they will likely not point out that you are 100% liable if the fraudster doesn't make a mortgage payment on time. YOU are responsible for the payments, and the fraudster can leave you hanging on a whim, even if he assumes the mortgage from you.

When you allow someone to assume a mortgage from you, if that person defaults, you are still on the hook. If the mortgage goes into default, YOU are the one responsible for the foreclosure, YOUR credit will be ruined, and it is YOU who may be forced into bankruptcy. Any agreement or contract which you may sign with the fraudster which you believe will protect you from liability will be **100% unenforceable** because it is a contract which agrees to participate in a crime.

The fraudster may promise that he will take all the responsibility, and may even offer a contract which appears to assume the responsibility, but the criminal knows full well that the contract is non-binding. **Criminal contracts are not contracts at all, and you will be completely unprotected.**

Another form of mortgage fraud happens when a **false market value** has been created. Here is an actual true story of what happened to one of my clients:

Elaine responded to an advertisement for affordable condo units which were converted from a three-story apartment building. The seller was a small-time developer who converted the building and was selling the units by owner. Of the 16 units, the first four of the units were sold by a professional Realtor. These sales created an MLS record of the transactions so the public would have access to the SOLD prices of those units. When Elaine was shown the prices which the first four units sold for, she was convinced the price of the unit she was interested in was a fair price.

When she spoke about the condo unit with her son, Adam, something didn't seem quite right to him. Adam urged his mom to call me for a second opinion of price before she went ahead with the deal. Adam was a past client of mine, and I was happy to provide some free help to his mom with the purchase. I took down all the pertinent information from her, and told Elaine I'd get back to her the next day after I had a chance to do some digging.

After several hours of careful research and analysis, I was convinced the price of $125,000.00 was far too high for the unit she was interested in. At the most, a condo like hers should have sold for $75,000.00 in the market at that time. When I called her to share what I found, she was insistent *that I was wrong and that the sale price of the four other units were proof of the value. I acknowledged those sales, but shared with her that something seemed fishy about those sales and that no other units in the city supported their sale prices. I also shared with her that the neighbourhood was known to be a high crime area. Regardless, Elaine disagreed and was adamant it was both a great area and a great building.*

Elaine thanked me for my advice but decided to proceed regardless, and without representation from a Realtor. I let her know my door was open and would provide help free of charge if she had any questions, but she didn't take me up on my offer.

Six months after she moved into her condo, she decided she had to sell.

As it turned out, the building was full of loud, obnoxious tenants and her unit was the only one that was owner-occupied. Her car had been broken into three times since she moved in, the police were often rushing into the building, and she felt unsafe walking to and from her car.

Elaine called me in tears, asking me what she could list her condo at. Again, I did a full market evaluation, and at best her condo could only sell for about $75,000.00. The market had not changed and she had clearly over-paid for her unit.

When I started to investigate how the first four units could have possibly sold for such high prices, what I discovered was evidence of mortgage fraud.

As it turned out, the Realtor who sold the units used straw buyers who were paid by the developer, then the developer assumed the mortgages from the straw buyers. In essence, the developer sold the units to himself. I found proof of this and discovered he used his own family members as straw buyers.

These transactions created both fraudulent funds for the developer, as well as created a falsely inflated market Elaine was devastated.

She couldn't bear to live in the building anymore, but couldn't afford to keep the place without renting it out. Elaine moved out and found a renter for her place, but the rent was never paid on time and the unit was constantly being damaged. Elaine had to get a roommate and a second job in order to stay afloat. Elaine's only option was to keep the condo until the market value increased enough that she could sell the unit and at least break even. ***It was four long years before she was able to finally put the unit up for sale and break even.***

Section Notes

What was my greatest take-away from this section?

What do I need to remember about this section?

13

Pre-sale Renovations and R.O.I. (**R**eturn **O**n **I**nvestment)

Dumb money vs Smart money

When I'm looking for a great investment property to flip, one of the key factors I'm looking for is what I call the "Dumb Money". The more dumb money which has been invested into a home prior to sale, the better house-flipping potential the home has.

Dumb money is the money you invest without receiving a positive return on your investment. In other words, renovations which simply do NOT increase the value of your home more than the amount spent. Spending the dumb money may help your house sell more quickly, but it does not help you net more profit.

Some examples of Dumb Money are:

- Furnace
- Fence
- Deck
- Windows
- Landscaping
- Concrete driveways
- Any poorly done renovations
- Finishing the basement
- Drywalling the garage
- Roof (on a case-by-case basis)

Any of the above are almost guaranteed to result in losing profit instead of making profit. That being said, all of the above will increase the marketability of your home and help to reduce your time on market.

Some items just can't be ignored and really should be done, regardless of the net ROI.

When buyers are interested in your home, the #1 thing that will turn them off is the **hassle factor**. Doing necessary renovations involve more than a significant cost, they involve the hassle of calling contractors, getting quotes, taking time off work, and hoping it's done right the first time... which it often isn't. Reducing the hassle factor makes your home more attractive to potential buyers.

The biggest one on the list which needs to be done is the **roof**. It's a significant expense, and taints the image of the entire home as appearing to be in a state of disrepair.

Selling a home with a roof which obviously needs to be replaced puts the seller in a poor negotiation position. Although from an appraisal standpoint, a new roof only adds to your home on a dollar in, dollar out basis, it still makes your home far more attractive to any buyer.

Second in line is your furnace. If your furnace is more than 20 years old, it will be a significant hindrance when trying to sell your home. With the price of natural gas constantly rising, buyers are looking for high efficient furnaces, not old clunkers.

In many cases, buyers ask to review the last six months of utility bills as a buyers condition in the purchase contract.

Hot water tanks are not on this list because they are only about $1,100.00 installed and, if new, can add a lot of value to a home. This is because hot water tanks only last about ten years, and a new one takes the focus off of other items – like an old clunker furnace.

"Finishing the basement" is on this list because even if you do it yourself, you have to count your time as an expense. Unless you are a professional renovator, finishing a basement takes a LOT of time, and even the most handy homeowners will likely only break even on their investment when they factor in their time spent on the project.

What I've found is that the R.O.I. of finishing your own basement is usually the same as paying yourself roughly $5.00/hour. In many cases, the investment in the basement will be more than you can receive in the increased sale price of your home, meaning a negative R.O.I. (Return On Investment).

I often recommend that only the basement's parameter walls be wired, insulated, dry-walled, taped and painted. This way the remainder of the basement renovations will seem much less overwhelming to buyers, plus it leaves the floor plan open to be chosen by the buyer.

The Smart Money

Most people believe that **Kitchens and Bathrooms** (K&B) are the best investment you can make to increase the value of your home... and most people would only be partially correct.

Kitchens and Bathrooms are magical places where nearly limitless amounts of money can disappear without a trace.

It's absolutely true that K&B are a great place to invest; however, extreme caution must be exercised prior to engaging in those renovations.

Here is what **NOT** to do with K&B on the average single family home (Luxury Homes have some different rules and are case-by-case):

- Over-spend on custom, high-end carpentry or cabinets
- Do it yourself, unless you have experience and are very confident in your ability to produce on a professional level
- Decorate to YOUR own personal tastes; visit modern show homes to see how they decorate
- Go half way; if you start, you have to finish
- Have different counters / sinks / fixtures in every bathroom
- Have bathroom flooring which isn't rated for bathroom moisture
- Board bathroom walls without using the board which is moisture rated, e.g.: green drywall, or concrete board

Paint is Cheap

If... and ONLY if you are really good at painting, this is the best pre-sale renovation you can do. Regardless of what the rest of the home looks like, if all the walls have had the dings and chips repaired and have been properly painted with modern colour choices, you almost certainly will have a positive return on investment. If you are NOT a great painter, hiring a professional who has great references is highly recommended. A fresh coat of paint throughout the home gives a very positive overall impression.

Make sure to look up! The ceiling is the best place for you to start painting and is definitely not to be skipped. A fresh coat of paint on the ceiling goes a long way to making the home feel brighter and cleaner. If there are any old water stains or obvious ceiling repairs, be sure to have a professional re-do that area of the ceiling so the repair is invisible.

CAUTION: IF THERE IS AN UNDERLYING LEAKING ISSUE, THIS MUST BE PROPERLY REPAIRED OR DISCLOSED TO THE BUYER... OR BOTH

Make sure to look down! Baseboards are often overlooked but must not be ignored. There are seven rules to baseboards and door casings:

1. They must be installed correctly
2. They must not show any gaps at the joints (dap / caulking is your friend)
3. They must be in good shape
4. The tops of the baseboards must be caulked, ensuring there is not a gap between the baseboard and the walls
5. They must be modern and match your door casings
6. No shortcuts! The job MUST look professional. There are many molding accessories offered at hardware stores for amateur carpenters who don't know how to correctly cut angles and return mitres; these accessories often make the job look amateur and don't fool most buyers

7. They must be 100% complete – all nail / staple holes must be filled, mouldings must be painted and caulked, and all the mouldings in the home must match; at the very least, the mouldings should match on each individual level

The MOST common D.I.Y. (Do It Yourself) carpentry in homes is baseboards and door casings (mouldings). Even though this is classified as finishing carpentry, wanna-be carpenters try to save a few dollars by tackling mouldings on their own.

Very few D.I.Y. moulding installations look professional, and if they don't look professional, you have just wasted your time and money. Most buyers will feel a need to replace them.

If you follow the rules above, chances are you'll invest your renovation money wisely.

If you have a local Realtor in your area that is well versed at **Pre-Renovation Consultations**, you would be well served to consult with that Realtor prior to buying your materials. Once your renovations are complete, have the same Realtor do a **Post-Renovation Review** prior to you placing your home on the market. The Post-Renovation review will ensure the right steps were taken and that you have not missed addressing any key factors.

Section Notes

What was my greatest take-away from this section?

What do I need to remember about this section?

14

Roofing Rescue

by Larry Metz

Why should I replace my roof?

Roofing materials don't change at the same intense speed which technology does; however, in the 15+ years since your roof was installed, the industry has made some big improvements and has introduced a larger variety of product choices. We live in a culture which is constantly moving toward being more efficient and cost effective in all areas of life, and the roofing industry is no exception.

Replacing your roof gives you the opportunity to update the existing material with a newer, more proficient product which has been tried, tested and proven to be both reliable and long lasting. Additionally, experienced and skilled contractors will understand the current products on the market. Being knowledgeable about all available products is advantageous because it empowers the contractor to help the homeowner choose the right product which matches your individual situation. A quality, professional contractor will cover all the details, from proper amounts of ventilation or appropriate underlay which can significantly extend the life of your roof, to the cosmetic curb appeal which best compliments the overall look of your home.

Most people will only replace their roof once during their ownership, and if you've been living in your home for more than a year, you likely know what the common weather patterns are in your area. Climate can be a great determining factor when choosing your new roofing material. If your home is often exposed to strong winds, you'll not only want a product which has the best fastening technology but you must also be confident that there are extra steps performed during installation to help prevent any future wind damage.

You need the right roof for the right situation!

Another compelling reason to replace your roof is resale value. Most homeowners know that buying an older home means renovations will come with it, but no one wants to deal with needing an expensive new roof six months after moving in.

Other than the obvious hideousness of an old roof, there could be other issues lurking in the shadows of your attic or under your shingles. Replacing the roof before selling your home can save you from nasty surprises after the **buyer's home inspector** checks out your attic and shingles. Putting your house on the market with confidence helps provide you with peace of mind.

How do I know it's time for a new roof?

There are several signs that will show if your roof needs replacement or repairs:

- Curling or cracked shingles
- Granular loss
- Patches where you can see the black asphalt below
- Water leaks
- Uneven roof line due to warped roof sheeting

Occasionally, fixing a leaky roof is only a matter of replacing a few shingles. More often, missing shingles are an indicator the roof may be at the end of its life cycle and that the shingles are no longer secured by the fasteners. In this case, it is necessary to replace the entire roof.

If your house still has the original roof, the age of the house can be an indication that it's time to replace the roof. Are the houses in your neighbourhood getting new roofs? This can also be a good indicator.

Be a storm watcher! After a significant hail storm or wind storm, it is important to pay attention to your roof. If you are not certain of what to look for, many roofing companies are willing to inspect your roof for a reasonable fee or even for free.

Know your deductible. Insurance companies can change the rules of what they are willing to cover for a claim of a damaged roof. Be sure you call your insurance company once a year to receive an update on how or if they provide coverage for hail or wind damage.

Section Notes

What was my greatest take-away from this section?

What do I need to remember about this section?

15

Top Eight "Must Knows" About Flooring

by Cory Alger

Home renovations are a very popular discussion among Realtors, interior designers, and property owners looking to invest in their home. People think that if they renovate their home before selling, they can increase the asking price enough to cover the expenses, plus put a little extra in their pocket. Truth be told… they're right! "Pre-sale renovations" is a large part of the "renovation" category, and who wouldn't want to make a little extra cash when they sell their home? Invest $20,000.00 worth of renovations and up your asking price $30,000.00. Seems like easy money, right? Well, let's just say many property owners and designers have made mistakes along the way and what they put in, they did not get out. Some of the biggest and most costly mistakes you can make during pre-sale renovations is with your choice of flooring. With so many different products, manufacturers and colors, it's hard to know which choice is the right choice.

I'm going to try clear a few things up for you. These are my top eight most important flooring topics to be aware of when considering buying or selling a property:

1. Get a professional! I know that today's world loves to DIY, and you can take flooring installation courses at hardware stores or read the directions on the box and rent the tools they recommend, but ultimately you will not get the same results as someone who is trained in the industry and has skill with a saw. Also, there are a few "key tools" that the box instructions and courses don't tell you about. Don't be fooled by the dozens of hammer swingers that claim to be flooring installers. They will undercut the market drastically just to get jobs. Ensure the person or company you hire has liability insurance, professional grade tools, experience and testimonials. Anything less, and you may very well regret going with the lowest bidder.

2. Sand & refinish or rip out and replace. Today's hardwood market consists of two main types of hardwood floors. Site Finished or Pre-Finished. Site finished requires a solid hardwood plank, whereas pre-finished can be solid or engineered hardwood. With a site finish installation, the client will usually have to leave the premises for a few days or weeks (depending on the size of the job), so the installers / finishers can have room to work and the floor has time to cure after the final coat. The cost of a site finished floor is quite a bit more than having a prefinished floor installed. One, because of your added costs for finding accommodations while the renovation is taking place, and two, you're paying for the installation of the hardwood as well as the sand and finish. Even if you have a site finished floor already and you want to only sand and refinish, the cost will often still be as high as replacing with a pre-finished floor. That is, provided you have hired a **professional** that knows what he is doing. Don't forget the old saying, "Cheap work isn't good and good work isn't cheap". That being said, a quality site finished floor will add more value to your home than any other type of floor. Pre-finished floors, however, have become very popular with their ease of installation, the ability to change boards if you scratch or damage any, and their endless colors, textures, widths and thicknesses that can fit any home renovation. Don't get me wrong, there are still expensive prefinished floors out there, but for the masses, this is usually the more affordable option when trying to stay in the hardwood category.

The downfall to a pre-finished hardwood is that the quality of the floor depends more on the manufacturer than it does the company installing the product. Not by much, but if the wood is warped, it makes it hard to lay a straight floor and puts a lot of pressure on the boards because you're flexing them into place. This causes pressure cracks in boards and can make your floor sound like bubble wrap when you walk on it. Also, you can have hairline gaps between boards from where the floor didn't get sucked together tight enough (usually around closing walls and cabinets where you can't fit the bigger nailers). If the stain is blotchy / streaky, the installers are required to remove these boards and you may end up having to pick up more product to make up for the ones they have removed, costing you even more money. If the tongue and grooves aren't milled properly, you can get a lot of squeaking from having too much movement between the boards. As well, the floor may not look completely flat because boards will peak between joints when nailed. Quality products will be milled so the tongues fit tight and the boards are the same widths at both ends. These issues are not as common in site finished floors because gaps can be filled and sanded, and the finish quality is determined by the contractor's skill level / products he chooses to work with. So, when buying pre-finished hardwood, always remember you get what you pay for, and expect to have a few of these issues when you find (what looks to be) a great deal.

3. Humidity control is a must! If you do not have a working **furnace humidifier** in your home, I strongly suggest getting one and having it professionally installed and tested before thinking of hardwood for your choice of flooring. Humidity levels in the home determine how your floor is going to react during the changing seasons. When it's cold outside, your furnace will run more often and can dry out a floor dramatically. This causes gapping, delamination and cracks in the finish of the product. If you have too much humidity in the home, solid hardwood will expand and create what we call "cupping or crowning".

4. Cupping will happen when moisture is introduced directly into the product, whether that be from the top of the product (spills or leaks from fridge lines, toilets, dog bowls, etc.) or from the bottom of the product through the subfloor (basement leaks, cracked foundations, etc.). Moisture gets trapped between the boards, and the edges will expand, pushing against the other boards and forcing it up.

5. Crowning happens when moisture is introduced indirectly to the top side of the floor (steam from a shower in a bathroom without a fan or water leaks in another area of the home that raises the general relative humidity). The center of the board will expand rather than the edges. This can also happen when a floor has direct contact with water, the product cups on its edges, and you do not allow enough time for the product to dry out properly before re-sanding and finishing. If you sand the cupping flat then the floor has a chance to dry out, the edges will now be lower than the centers. Small indications of cupping and crowning should be considered normal for solid wood floors if you have dramatic changes in weather in a short period of time.

6. Engineered hardwood will also be affected by humidity levels. With too little humidity, engineered products can "de-laminate" which is where the real hardwood top will separate from the wood core that it has been attached to. Generally, this happens in high traffic areas because the glue that bonds the two dries out and starts to crack with continual movement. This problem can only be fixed by removing and replacing the damaged boards. **Do I need a moisture barrier underlay?** The answer is YES! The only product you don't necessarily need moisture protection for is Luxury Vinyl because the product itself is already waterproof. Not every manufacturer requires you to use an underlay with a moisture barrier, but my argument is, *Why wouldn't you?* The cost difference between moisture protected and not moisture protected is usually insignificant when it comes to the total cost of the job. As well, there are many added benefits to having such things. An example would be if you have a leak on your engineered hardwood, laminate or cork flooring, a moisture protected underlay can help keep the moisture from reaching into the subfloor and creating an even bigger structural issue. If you purchase a vinyl plank product that is mounted on an HDF Core, even though the vinyl itself will not be affected by moisture, the High-Density Fiber Core will. I've seen many cases where a moisture barrier was not used, and a rise in temperature caused the vinyl on the top of the product to expand while the HDF Core shrunk because of the lack of moisture in the subfloor itself (caused by the rising temperature with no humidity control). The subfloor sucked the moisture right out of the product, causing it to pull apart from itself and essentially wrecking the locking mechanism of the product. This can happen to most products, including laminate, cork and engineered hardwood. Using an underlay with a moisture barrier will mitigate this type of transfer and allow it to happen at an acceptable rate. If gluing or nailing down a hardwood floor, the same rule applies. Make sure you are using a NWFA approved paper or adhesive with a moisture barrier. It will make for a long lasting, quiet floor that will fetch you "top dollar" when it comes time for re-sale.

7. Make sure you acclimate your product before installation. The most common flooring issues can usually be linked back to a lack of Acclimation. Acclimation is when you let your product sit in the installation areas of the home so it can adjust to its surrounding climate. Standard acclimation timeframe is usually 48 hours. When dealing with hardwood products, I always recommend at least five days, but always follow what the manufacturer recommends for time and how to stack your product for proper air flow. The levels of humidity you acclimate to is also very important. If you acclimate and install a laminate floor in the springtime, your home's humidity levels can be up in the 50% – 65% range due to rain, melting snow, etc. Once those humidity levels drop back to where your house usually sits, 30% - 40%, (maybe even 20% if you have no furnace at all or use electric baseboard heaters), your floor is going to shrink dramatically, causing a lot of movement and will probably start to separate. You want to install your flooring at a humidity level that is easiest to maintain all year round and try not to let it fluctuate more than 10% in either direction for extended periods of time.

8. Read and understand your warranty. There is a reason that I talk about moisture issues / prevention and maintaining humidity levels in your home. Almost all issues with a floor caused by humidity or moisture will NOT be covered by your product's manufacturing warranty. That's right! And if you can't prove that you have been doing everything necessary to maintain your floor, good luck getting a claim approved. This also goes for installing products in areas they shouldn't be; for example laminate in a bathroom, solid hardwood in a basement, etc. Most manufacturing warranties are "limited warranties" and generally apply to finishes and discoloration.

Here is an example of a typical laminate warranty:

Laminated Flooring Warranty

- Check the dates on the boxes; if you have different lots, make sure they are from the same color and that they are compatible
- Make sure the product conforms to the sample, and that it matches the choice and the requirements of the consumer
- Boards with faults should not be installed
- An installed floor is considered accepted by the consumer
- You must test the floor moisture before installing it (must not exceed 9%)
- You must test the ambient humidity (must be stable between 35%-55%)

- To clean your laminate flooring, apply a floor cleaner directly to a cloth, never directly on the floor
- Install felts under the legs of the furniture to protect the floor

Our Guarantee

- Ensures that the color of the floor will not fade
- The warranty is applicable to the original owner and is not transferable

The warranty does not cover

- All problems due to improper installation
- Animal urine damage
- Discoloration due to excessive temperatures and/or sunlight
- Problems due to excessive humidity from household appliances, leaks, water damage or floods
- Damage caused during renovations and/or construction
- No labor is covered by this warranty

As you can see, the manufacturer's warranty doesn't really cover a whole lot. That's why it's up to you as the consumer to educate yourself and cover your own butt. It's also good to remember that flooring warranties are non-transferable, meaning if you sink a bunch of money into a new floor before you sell your home, the warranty will be void for the person buying it, even if it's brand-new! Which brings me to my next point...

8. Don't spend a bunch of money redoing things that people are going to redo anyway. If the laminate or cork floor in your home is in rough shape, don't replace it with another laminate floor and expect it to raise the value of your house much. You'll be lucky if it pays for the renovation and is worth the time and headache. Ever heard "go big or go home"? If you're going to replace your floor only to turn around and sell it, make sure it's going to be worth it, not just for you but for the consumer as well. Know your target market and make choices based around that knowledge. If you live by a school, a vinyl floor could be seen as "value" because it works great with kids and pets. If you live in a higher end of town, replacing your old tile floor with new laminate or vinyl might be seen as a downgrade. Maybe the buyer would like a tile floor and now sees an added expense that they may have to remove your floor to get back to what fits their vision. You're also limiting your demographic to someone who likes the same things as you. Not everyone wants a dark floor, wood grain, or wide plank flooring. A key to a quick sale is for people to be able to see themselves in that home. Also, the smaller the market, the longer your house is going to sit there, which just adds costs for marketing and more of your time wasted.

9. If possible, always check the vent holes. You can save yourself a lot of headache when planning for a renovation by simply looking in your floor vents. You'll find out things like:

- **How thick the floor you are wanting to replace is.** Many people shop for flooring products without ever looking at what thickness of floor they need to match the old one! If you buy too thin, you run into issues with baseboard heights / paint lines or faded stain lines around cabinets and gaps around undercut door-jams. If you buy too thick, your doors may need to be trimmed, your appliances won't fit back in their holes, or floors you're butting up to now need clunky moldings to cover the height difference. And don't forget to calculate for the type and thickness of underlay you are going to use.

- **How many times has my site-finished floor been sanded, and is there enough left to do it again?** A lot of people don't realize that site-finished floors, though most start at ¾" thickness, can only be sanded a handful of times before you will start to expose the heads of the nails / cleats securing the product. You could get stuck paying a company for a job they can't finish, and end up removing and replacing anyways. If you're buying a home, this is definitely something to look for because how can a hardwood floor have value when it's pretty much useless? Keep in mind that there are other factors that will play into how much wood needs removed. For example, thickness of finish, how deep the stain goes, if you are transitioning from dark to light, etc. If you're within 1/8" from top of board to top of the tongues, I would consult a professional before making any choices.

- **What type of substrate am I dealing with?** If you're wanting a full spread, glue-down product (vinyl or engineered hardwood), concrete substrates usually don't require a ton of prep work. If you want it installed on a wood substrate, you now have additional costs of putting an extra sheathing layer down. You're not allowed to full spread glue products to structural wood substrates because in the event of a leak, removing that product will ruin the structural integrity of your floor. If too much damage has occurred, you could end up replacing the original subfloor as well. Did you know that particle board is not a suitable substrate for a nail down hardwood? If the previous contractor used it to sheathe for a floating floor, you will have to rip it out and re-sheet with plywood before installing any type of nail down product.

- **Which way are the floor joists running in my home?** For products like hardwood, direction of floor joists determines direction of the floor. Installing hardwood across the joists adds to durability and structural strength of the floor, as well as providing a flatter / less wavy look as foundations shift in the seasons. If you want to change the direction of your floor, a minimum ½" sheathe must be added to your original subfloor for support. Not completing this step will almost always void your manufacturer's warranty.

- **How many layers of floor am I dealing with?** You may be looking at buying a home and thinking, "I can renovate this, no problem; it's just a click laminate or vinyl floor." Well, if you don't look in the vents, you could be in for a lot more than you bargained for. I've seen homes with laminate on top of hardwood on top of linoleum on top of more linoleum. You could cost yourself thousands of dollars in unforeseen issues. Also, you need to pray you don't ever have a flood because the time and money it takes to rip all that out and make it workable again will drive your insurance premiums through the roof, as well as be a huge inconvenience for you and your family if you have to try and live there while the construction takes place.

Section Notes

What was my greatest take-away from this section?

What do I need to remember about this section?

16

Home Staging Essentials

The overall goal of home staging is to create an environment where the potential buyers can imagine themselves happily living in the home.

The **4 main obstacles** to people imagining themselves living in your home are:

- **Disrepair**
- **Lack of cleanliness**
- **Clutter**
- **Personalized decor (ownership stamp)**

1. **Disrepair** taints the entire home with a negative perception. The more disrepair in your home, the more powerful the negative perception is to potential buyers.

2. **Cleanliness** is essential. A lack of cleanliness makes a home feel as if it is in disrepair. This includes wiping all

marks off of cabinets and walls, and cleaning all appliances.

3. **Clutter** distorts the perception of the size of the rooms, makes a home feel dirty, and impairs a person's ability to imagine their OWN furniture being placed in the home.

4. **Personalized decor** creates a stamp of ownership on the home which declares, "This is MY house, not YOUR house"!

Examples of Personalized Decor are:

- Excessive family photos
- Unique or dated furnishings
- Odd colour choices
- Children's heights recorded on doorframes
- Clutter of any sort, but especially on countertops
- Bathroom clutter
- Pet beds or pet accessories
- Clothes not being put away
- Coats on coat racks instead of in the closet
- Shoes / boots not in closets
- Disrepair, lack of cleanliness, and clutter also add to the "ownership stamp", and greatly hinder a buyer's ability to imagine themselves having your home as THEIR home
- Unpleasant odours e.g.: litterbox, moth balls, cigarette smoke, strong air fresheners, sports equipment, teenager's rooms, spicy cooking, etc.

- Awards / trophies / certificates which are on display
- Sports team paraphernalia (especially if the buyers cheer for the OTHER team)
- Animal heads / taxidermy

Hiring a professional Home Stager should be a serious consideration for those who wish to get top dollar for their home. Staging your home is both an art and a science. Certified decorators and designers have the knowledge to create a space which is the most inviting to potential buyers.

17

Major Marketing Mistakes

Truth in marketing matters. If you over-promise and under deliver, you'll not be helping your cause. Here are some quick tips for what NOT to do:

- Do NOT sell your home like it's a used car. Features and Benefits can be included, but only if they are either RARE, highly desirable, or both

- Do NOT try to appeal to EVERYONE; understand which market segment is most likely to find your home attractive, and speak directly to them

- Do NOT abuse words like "amazing, incredible, spectacular"; if you over-promise, the buyer's perception will be tainted

- Do NOT sound just like everyone else who is trying to sell their home; ensure the written description has a creative way to **STAND OUT** from the crowd

- Do NOT price your home with the standard 999 as the last three numbers in the price; 999 appears arbitrary and wide open to negotiation

- Do NOT ignore pricing blocks when you choose to sell your home via the MLS or any other search engine; people generally shop in 50 or 100 thousand dollar price blocks, so if you are priced one price block too high, your property will only be viewed by people who are interested in homes which are nicer or larger than yours

- Do NOT guess your square footage because even if you have blueprints, they may not be reliable for measurements, and don't rely on a previous listing sheet or the measurements of anyone other than a measurement professional who is not only familiar with RMS standards but also carries Errors and Omissions insurance; if your ACTUAL square footage is less than your advertised square footage, you could be held liable and open yourself up for a lawsuit

Section Notes

What was my greatest take-away from this section?

What do I need to remember about this section?

18

Social Media Matters

by Julie Boake

Marketing your home

Back in the day, Realtors would put a sign on the lawn and the neighbourhood would spread the news of anyone moving. Now, in the age of modern tools and technology, the reach is, literally, worldwide.

1. Listen to your Realtor. And no, I am not getting paid to say that. After working with many Realtors marketing homes, one of the most costly things a home seller can do is fail to listen, so at the very least carefully consider the advice of the professionals giving it.

Marketing is about:

1-Product

2-Placement

3-Promotion
4-Price

In real estate, when selling a house, these are amplified. If you do all of the promotion in the world but your price is misaligned with the market, you are wasting your money and time promoting your home. If you have a great home but fail to get it (honestly) ready for sale, your product falls short and your price will be questioned.

Product

Get your home ready – People are visual creatures. Make your bed, clean up the scuffs and freshen your home. There is a reason why staged homes sell, on average, far higher than homes that have not been staged. Spend the money on professional photography. You get one chance to capture the curiosity of your audience.

Promotion

Promote well – Have you ever gone window shopping and ended up buying? Yes, that happens with homes as well. People fall in love with the vision of the lifestyle they will have with YOUR home, so show it. Online (social media) is a powerful tool and more and more people are being enticed to buy something from seeing it online, not to mention the power of capturing the relocation audience. Share your listing with your friends and don't be shy about asking them to also share it. You never know who it may reach!

When your Realtor pops the sign in the lawn, you can count on them to do everything, but you have a powerful reach as well, so why not utilize both of your collective audiences to sell your home? From your Realtor's point of view, they will highlight the features in a factual sense. This is their job, to help your home meet the criteria that buyers are looking for. This helps fill the MLS and the check boxes that buyers have.

As the seller, you can sell the lifestyle. Create the dream, remember all of the reasons why you loved your home and make someone else fall in love with it. For example, cups of coffee on the deck in the morning, bubble baths in your great soaker tub… sell the lifestyle dream.

Placement

Social media – You have friends and your friends have friends, so by also using your reach, you are bound to be six degrees of separation from your home buyer. Highlight and ask people to share that you are selling your home. If you think social media is only for young kids, it's not. There are multiple platforms, each serving a purpose and attracting a different market. Know your prospective buyer and ensure that you and your Realtor are advertising on that platform.

Make sure to use hashtags; not just the standard (#realestate, #homeforsale) but consider adding in your location and community (#calgary, #Inglewoood) and any specific features about your home that you think will target someone that is bound to love your home (#gardening, #chefskitchen).

One of the aspects people don't talk about is the 'Rant' pages on social media. If there are constant rants about a community, these can affect the perception of the community that your home may be in. People will ask questions and solicit advice, so a lot of negative press (i.e.: crime, bad schools, etc.) can be a red flag for people looking to make a purchase.

Before you list, know that the internet is a powerful tool and people will google and search the area. If you have taken pictures of crime, neighbour issues, decrepit or messes in the area, it may tag the location, so be sure to delete any incriminating images from your social media and tags.

Newspapers and traditional media – While these carry value, they are not the leading source of advertising for all demographics. While you may ask your Realtor to publish in these mediums, know that they do not always have the power and reach that they used to have.

MLS/Realtor.ca – This is a valuable tool. Many people browse realtor.ca and get alerts from signing up to Realtor pages for listings in their preferred areas. This is generally an automatic placement for any home.

Price – While a home purchase can be an emotional one, price does factor in. If the buyer's Realtor tells a prospect about the comparable homes in the community and your price is not in line or deemed a "good value", this can turn off buyers. Alternatively, if your home is priced well below average, this can make prospective buyers wonder if there is something wrong with the property. Heed the advice of your Realtor when selecting your price.

Section Notes

What was my greatest take-away from this section?

What do I need to remember about this section?

19

The LOVE Meter

Congrats, your house just hit the market! Your niche marketing message is awesome, there is a flurry of activity in the first week with several showings, and you're fully expecting at least three offers to come rolling in... but they don't. Instead, the showings grind to a halt and the crickets are singing you a tune. What the heck happened? It all looked so promising in the beginning!

ANSWER: The love meter drained under 7/10 when your prospective buyers toured your home.

Getting someone interested enough to view your home is a great achievement, but it's only half the battle. Once they are in the door, you can't under-deliver on the promises your marketing made.

- If you have taken professional photos of the home when it was staged then the buyer walks in to see clutter and mess, the love meter will drain
- If you promised new, professional renovations but the renovations were clearly DIY, the love meter will drain
- If there are chips in the baseboards, scuffs on the walls, tears in the carpet, disrepair of any sort, the love meter will drain
- If there is a 6' X 12' family photo of all of you in a hot-tub, the love meter will drain (I've actually seen this)
- If I can smell your cat's litterbox...
- If you have a fridge full of magnets with family photos...
- If your teenager's bedroom looks like a... well, like a teenager's bedroom...
- If your kitchen counters are jam-packed with appliances...

- If you make it difficult for buyers to schedule a viewing...

You only have one chance to catch the hearts of the buyers. If you expect the buyer to see past these things, I'm sorry, they just can't. I can because I've been bestowed with Realtor-Vision, but I'm in the minority.

To get top dollar for your home, there are a hundred little things that need to be done right the first time. The one thing which you have complete control over is the condition of your home when it is being shown. All those little jobs you've been putting off need to get done if you're to get the highest possible selling price.

The information in this book will go a long way to helping you to keep the love meter above the critical 70% level. If you achieve this goal, you will maintain a stronger negotiation position, which results in making more money on the sale of your home.

Section Notes

What was my greatest take-away from this section?

What do I need to remember about this section?

20

Showing Your Home to Potential Buyers... How NOT to Do It

Netflix has a crazy, dark comedy called "The Santa Clarita Diet". Two of the main characters are "typical" Realtors, portrayed in the same silly way in which Hollywood normally portrays my profession. While showing homes, the characters point out all of the features and benefits of the home with feigned enthusiasm, doing their utmost to create interest in the minds of the potential buyers. It's the same silly stereotype every time a Realtor is depicted in Hollywood, with the agent portrayed as an emptyheaded huckster who just wants to get the house sold to anyone who they can pressure into buying it.

Imagine your home is a used car lot... then put yourself in the shoes of the buyer. Do you REALLY want to get their defenses up by using the same tactics which you hate having used on you? Even if you're really good at traditional feature and benefit selling (nobody is good at it because it doesn't work anymore), taking this approach will do nothing to get your house sold, and may actually cause you harm.

What if you wrangle the buyers into writing an offer which you both can live with? Isn't that all you want to have happen? NOPE. Getting an offer is a nice start, but if you don't have a qualified offer, all you're doing is taking your house off the market for a week or two, just to find out that UH OH!!! their financing fell through!!! Bummer. Now you've missed out, lost up to two weeks of precious time, and have to start from the beginning.

So, how could you have known? By NOT spending your time telling them all about your house, but instead spend your time getting to know THEM, their motivation and their situation.

- If they were pre-approved... when did that happen (they expire)?
- Who are they pre-approved with?
- What are the conditions of the pre-approval?
- Do they currently own a home which they have to sell in order to buy your home?
- Are they waiting for an inheritance for their down payment?
- Do they need a CMHC mortgage?

- Is an ex-spouse about to sue them for child support which would wipe out the down payment (I include this because it happened to a potential client)?
- Are they REALLY looking to buy or are they just preparing to sell on their own and want to check out the competition?
- WHEN do they want to be in a house by?

When you were showing them the house, did you ask them what they liked and what they didn't like? Did you ask them if there were any issues which could be a potential deal breaker? Without the right information, you don't know how strong their will is to complete the sale, much less what their financial capacity is.

Professional selling is all about COLLECTING information, not giving it.

- Know who they are
- what their motivations are
- and what their financial capacity is

They don't need you telling them about the workmanship of the home, they can decide for themselves what they like or dislike, and if the home is a good fit for their family.

Showing a home correctly means greatly decreasing your time on market and increasing your profits. It pays do get this one particular skill polished.

Even if people know which questions they should be asking, most people are simply too uncomfortable to ask questions which they feel may be overly invasive or awkward. Knowing HOW to ask is just as important as knowing WHAT to ask.

Don't be an inquisitor. If you sound like a lawyer cross-examining someone on the stand, the buyers will run for the door. Instead, follow this simple **three step process** and these **five main rules.**

The Process:

- Create rapport
- Start with non-invasive questions
- Gradually ask the more pointed questions... but ONLY if their body language, tone, and facial expressions give you the message that they are comfortable with your questions

The Rules:

- Never allow a one legged showing (where only one spouse or decision maker is present)
- Ensure your body language, tone and facial expressions are warm, welcoming and non-threatening
- Back off if you are making them uncomfortable
- At the end of the showing, always ask, "Are there any deal breakers that you saw?"
- Agree with them on what the next step should be, and don't easily accept, "I have to sleep on it."

Section Notes

What was my greatest take-away from this section?

What do I need to remember about this section?

21

Common Real Estate Myths

I see homeowners consistently making decisions based on bad information, resulting in the same costly mistakes over and over again. Most of these mistakes are due to the urban legends of real estate, which people tend to blindly believe.

- Summer is the best time to sell
- My home is worth more because it's "custom built"
- New windows are a good investment
- My sprinklers make my home worth more than the comparable properties
- I don't want to "give my house away"
- It's a great offer because it's a "cash deal"
- I just have to wait for the "right buyer" to come along
- Never take the first offer
- Open houses get homes SOLD

- Selling on my own means I will definitely save commissions
- My bank loves me and will provide me with the best rate
- I should refuse to respond to "low ball" offers
- If they don't ask, I don't have to tell
- If I am listed on the MLS through a "by owner" company, that's just as much exposure as being listed by a full time Realtor on the MLS
- All Realtors do is open doors and put the house on the MLS system
- A good Realtor personally brings buyers to the house

The list of fallacies goes on and on. If you believe in and act on two or more fallacies, you're very likely to lose a lot of money when you go to sell your home.

22

Crucial Negotiation Skills and Tactics

Can you sell ice to the Inuit? Can you sell sand in the middle of the Mojave Desert? If so, ignore this section. Ignore it, not because it won't be valuable to you, but because you will likely roll your eyes at the information I'm sharing.

I would NEVER sell sand in the Mojave or ice to an Inuit person for the simple reason that it is wrong to sell something to someone which they neither want nor need. If you don't care about selling ethics, then definitely skip this chapter completely.

For the rest of you who are still reading, I have some good news for you. Selling the old way doesn't work very well anymore. The general public has wised up to all the old, slimey tricks, and no longer tolerates them.

Negotiate with the fair tactics which I am about to share with you, and you will get the best deal possible... and you will be able to sleep soundly the following night. This section is NOT for greasy sales people, pushy bullies, or "know it alls". The tools shared in the section are based on world-renowned techniques which are used at even the highest end of the business world.

Mindset

A foundational component of your negotiation position is your mindset. It is your mindset which dictates your tone, and your choices of words and tactics. Old school sales training teaches to "overcome objections", which in reality means "argue with your client / customer". It's good to challenge a belief, but it's not a good idea to pick a fight.

If you choose to argue, the only potential winner is your ego, so I recommend avoiding an argument.

When you're selling your home on your own, **the buyer is your customer, not your opponent**. If you forget this fact, the chances are the negotiation will get hostile and you will not be in a position to negotiate the best possible price.

This is an excerpt on mindset from my book, *Why Not Me? the Keys to Unlock Your Power and Release Your Potential*.

Here is one key which was hugely important for me to understand. I used to argue with anyone – about anything.

I just couldn't tolerate an opinion that differed from my own. This stemmed from an unconscious belief that if my opinion mattered, I would matter. For me to be right, there had to be something right about me. If I could get someone to agree with my point of view, I would feel important and influential.

By convincing someone else, I felt that I was smarter than them and it just took some arguing to prove it! Once I realized that it wasn't about me and that my opinions were not weakened by contradictory opinions, I was then able to let go of a lot of anger.

Getting angry at the opinion of others is a sure sign of insecurity. *Other people's opinions are a product of who they are, so if I can't accept their opinions, then I can't accept them for who they are. We all have a right to believe anything we want to believe, regardless of what we believe is right or wrong.*

It is possible to respect an opinion without agreeing with it. Differences need to be respected.

This concept is transferable to any differences, whether it is differences in beliefs, lifestyle, culture, or physical appearance. We don't have to agree with or condone the differences in order to respect the rights of others to be different.

Opinions can be contagious, but there is no need to avoid being exposed to opinions or ideas which contradict our own. Opinions should never be considered to be a threat unless they are highly negative or filled with hate.

Religious wars have been and are now being fought for the sake of being "right". Believe in what you like and believe it as strongly as you like, just don't battle or go to war to protect your beliefs. It is people's actions that create a threat – not their beliefs. Let others believe what they wish. If you want your beliefs to be respected, you must also respect the beliefs of others, regardless of how silly or wrong you may think they are. You may go to war to protect your family, human rights, way of life, or sovereignty, but don't go just because someone has a different belief system from yours.

If you are secure in what you believe, there should never be cause to feel threatened by contradictory beliefs. If you believe that the entire universe was created in six days, there is no need to attack those who believe that it took billions of years to create the heavens and earth.

The truth is independent of our beliefs.

When the scientific community (the Church) believed that the world was flat, this belief was touted as an absolute fact. Anyone who said anything different (Galileo) was jailed or put to death as a heretic. Dissent equalled treason against the Church.

No matter how strongly the people believed that the world was flat, the world didn't get any flatter. It didn't matter how many people were punished for saying the world was round, the world still didn't get any flatter. The truth was and is that the world was and is a sphere.

The truth wasn't affected by the so-called "facts" of the day. The truth is independent of what we believe. By understanding that we really don't "know" much (if anything), we will then have the wisdom to take both new and old information with a grain of salt.

"The only true wisdom is in knowing that we know nothing." – Socrates

When people are confronted with an opinion which is way out of their comfort zone, they are quick to call others "crazy" for having that opinion. If an opinion is out of your comfort zone, it doesn't matter how true it is; you will find difficulty accepting it as truth. Just because something sounds "crazy" doesn't mean that it's not true.

This resistance to new information is known as "cognitive dissonance".

Imagine a UFO lands in your own backyard; an alien emerges from the craft, has a nice chat and cup of coffee with you, and then flies away.

If it happened, it happened, and there is no amount of denial that's going to change that. However, you will still be called a "crazy nut job" by most anyone to whom you tell the story. You could have a home video, still photos, and even a lock of hair from the alien, and it still wouldn't matter. A few more people might be convinced, but the majority will ignore the truth and find ways to discredit your evidence.

The easiest way to trivialize and discredit a story is to label it as "crazy". It takes maturity and self-confidence to be open to uncomfortable possibilities. For most people, making a lot of money is a very uncomfortable possibility. The idea that you are capable of far more than you ever thought possible is a very uncomfortable possibility, but it's true regardless of how uncomfortable you feel about it. The more open you are to the possibility that some of your beliefs might be self-limiting, the more able you will be to identify and remove those beliefs.

Also, if you are able to accept the possibility that you might not be "right", then you will have the ability to have much more respect for the uncomfortable opinions and beliefs of others. Just because something is uncomfortable to you doesn't mean that it isn't correct.

The stronger you hold onto the idea that others should agree with you, the smaller your world will be.

It's important to get comfortable with being uncomfortable. To learn anything, it means that you will have to accept that there is more for you to learn. Anytime we try something new, it is going to be uncomfortable since we haven't done it before. If you're not able to deal with the discomfort, then you will not be able to grow. Building your muscles works the same way. If you want to build your muscles and increase your strength, you must push yourself well past a level that is comfortable. If you don't go beyond what is comfortable, your muscles will not grow in either size or strength.

"Confidence comes not from always being right, but from not fearing to be wrong." –Peter T. McIntyre

Adopting this foundational mindset will allow you to connect with the person on the other side of the negotiation. By connecting with the other person, you will be able to listen to them closely enough to potentially hear an opportunity to adjust either the conditions or terms of the sale in such a way that you will negotiate a better price in return for adjusting those terms or conditions. Even if you are not successful in negotiating a better price, you will still create a more solid deal.

Deals can fall apart for no other reason than spite.

I've seen several instances where either a buyer or a seller changed their mind and killed the deal for no other reason than the other party offended them. It is to your advantage to keep the negotiation civil and positive as much as possible.

For more on negotiation strategy, consider buying the book *The Ten Commandments of Negotiation* by Stefan Aarnio. There is much more to negotiation than most people are aware.

Section Notes

What was my greatest take-away from this section?

What do I need to remember about this section?

23

Responding to a Purchase Offer

The Purchase Offer has been made!

YAY!!! All of your hard work and diligent planning has paid off! You have just received an offer, and you are now sitting down to review it. Typically, you will make the rookie mistake of jumping straight to the offer price and will put most of your attention on the price you will counteroffer at. By having your focus on the LAST item you should be looking at, you are missing out on all of the essentials. Rookie negotiators just focus on the price, not realizing there is often a monetary value related to the conditions and terms. People will often pay more to get the conditions and terms which best suit them.

Before you respond to the purchase offer, you must first understand the buyer's bargaining position!!!

Here is a list of what you need to know before evaluating the amount of the purchase offer.

- The possession date. Is it a date which works for you? Is it on a Friday? **How important is the possession date to the buyer?**
- The conditions and the condition date. Rarely should you allow more than ten business days for conditions. The longer the condition date, the longer your home is off the market. Deals fall apart, and if you accept this offer, your home will be off the market for the duration of the life of the conditions. Are the conditions reasonable?
- Is the offer subject to sale of the buyer's home? If so, you must find out the following:
- Is their home already listed?
- Is it listed by owner or by a Realtor? Realtor listed homes are far more likely to sell and usually sell more quickly.
- What is the current average D.O.M. (Days On Market)?
- What is the track record (list to sale ratio and average D.O.M.) of both the Realtor and the Brokerage which has it listed?
- Are they asking too much?
- How likely is it their home will sell quickly?
- How motivated are they to sell their home and buy your home?
- What issues may potentially pop up which would kill the deal?

- Are there any TERMS which have to be crossed out or amended? If so, what is the implication of those changes?
- Is there a clause in the Home Inspection condition which allows a non-licensed person to perform the inspection? If so, you will want to push back hard on that clause. When "Uncle Jimmy" the handyman does the inspection, he always finds issues which are not even there and makes mountains out of mole hills... every single time. You should fear Uncle Jimmy. He is NOT your friend. Uncle Jimmy is a deal killer, and you should not let him in your home.
- Subject to financing? Find out what you need to know about their financial position. If their credit or income is marginal, you may not want to risk accepting the deal. Also, you will want to know who is handling the mortgage. Is it a licensed mortgage broker or just a bank employee?
- How bad do they want the chattels (non-fixed items such as appliances, garden sheds, lawn tractors, shelving, etc.)?

Try to **negotiate the CONDITIONS and chattels before you negotiate the PRICE!** Remember that both the conditions and the chattels often carry a monetary value to the buyer. If you discover which conditions are the MOST important and which chattels are the most attractive to the buyer, make sure you give them everything they want. If you follow this advice, you will be in the best bargaining position possible when negotiating the final term of price. I have seen people pay an extra $10,000.00 just to get the possession date they wanted.

Most times, when chattels are included in the price, it's the seller who wins. Buyers will often pay top dollar for chattels when they are included in the mortgage.

Once you have gathered all the necessary information possible to ascertain the buyer's bargaining position, THEN it's time to evaluate the offer price and decide the best way to respond to it.

In the case of a low offer, NEVER refuse to respond to the deal because you are offended by the Low-Ball price. The way to respond to a Low-Ball is **not** by trying to play Hard-Ball.

Negotiation is a dance, not a fight. If they attempt to dominate the dance, do not take it personally.

Search for "Transactional Analysis" presentations on "YOUTUBE". Learn about the child, adult and parent ego states. Master these principles prior to entering negotiations.

When you get upset and turn the dance into a fight, the only winner will be your pride, not your profit margin. If your negotiation gets adversarial, both sides will often become stubborn. If one or both sides become stubborn, the chances of the deal falling apart before it starts are high, and the chance of you getting the best possible deal are very low.

Most people are not highly trained professional negotiators, and neither are most home buyers, so don't take it personally if they try to pound you into submission with a ridiculously low offer. Some people just have to try the low-ball, but they don't really mean it to be their bottom line.

Allow yourself to play the game, and pass the offer back and forth a couple of times to see how far they are willing to move. At the end of the day, if they don't reach your bottom line, you will just kill the deal anyway, which is fine. Be sure not to kill it without just cause.

Having buyers and sellers in the same room negotiating directly is almost always a bad thing when it comes to selling your home. People usually have a lot of emotional attachment and pride in their home, which makes them highly susceptible to becoming easily offended during the negotiation process. This is why I highly recommend learning "Transactional Analysis". By understanding which ego state you are in and which ego state the buyer is in, you can use your "adult" ego state to your advantage. **The better you are at maintaining your adult ego state, the more powerful you will be during the negotiations.**

One of the functions of having professional, third party representation is that it helps to keep the negotiation both professional and cordial (adult ego state). Once emotions get high, rationale gets low and poor decisions tend to be made.

If the negotiation isn't done right, even if the deal moves forward and your house sells, you may be open to future litigation. If you forget to dot an "I" or cross a "T", the buyer may be positioned to come at you after the fact to sue for what they believe is a loss. Even if it's a weak lawsuit, being sued is not a good time whether you win or not.

Future liability is another strong reason to keep the negotiation civil and avoid any arguments. People will do crazy things out of spite, and you don't want to be on the other end of a spiteful person who can afford a good lawyer.

The bottom line is, if you don't want a Realtor as the middle person, then give strong consideration to hiring a professional mediator who is well versed in real estate law. Selling a home is not like selling a used car, and the stakes are very high due to the significant dollar amount.

Success! You have an accepted offer... but now what?

First, understand that your house is NOT sold... not yet. I've often heard clients bragging about their home being sold when in fact it was only PENDING, otherwise known as "conditionally sold". I have seen shaky deals stay together and I've seen solid deals fall apart, so don't count your chickens before they are hatched.

Your job at this point in the process is to keep this deal together, which can often be the most difficult part of the entire process.

If you are selling on your own, this part of the process can be difficult. You will want to monitor the progress and results of the home inspection, appraisal, financing, and any other items which may be part of the conditions. As a homeowner, you won't have easy access to this information. When two Realtors are dealing with each other, they usually are open to sharing the required information, as they are both motivated to keep the deal together. Also, mortgage brokers usually have an open line of communication with their mutual clients' Realtor, but would not be able to communicate with the selling homeowner due to confidentiality rules. This leaves those who are selling by owner in the dark with their fingers crossed and hoping for the best.

Section Notes

What was my greatest take-away from this section?

What do I need to remember about this section?

24

Realtor Commissions are 100% Negotiable

Yes, really. Here is what you need to know about Realtor rates but probably don't.

*****DISCLAIMER*****
Neither the Author nor any of the contributing authors are claiming there is a "standard" commission rate.

Clients often look at me with stunned amazement and surprise when I tell them that commissions are not fixed but instead are totally negotiable. Also, they can be calculated on a percentage basis or as a flat fee.

In one conversation I had with a person who was selling by owner, I asked him if he was going to offer a fee for Realtors who bring a buyer. He replied, "You all charge the same thing, it's full pop or nothing!" By "full pop" he was referring to the most common rates for buyers agents in our Alberta market. This rate structure is so common that he assumed it was fixed in stone which, of course, it is not.

Imagine going to a used car lot and paying full sticker price without even trying to negotiate. Some lots are non-negotiable, but many still have some wiggle room if you simply choose to explore the possibility. It's the same with Realtors. Some will negotiate, others will not. For those who won't negotiate, you can either keep shopping for someone else or you can sell your home by owner. You have lots of options if you choose to look for them.

One friend of mine who is a business owner thinks about Realtor fees a little differently than most people. He wanted to make sure that both the listing agent and potential buyer's agents were incentified to bring him top dollar so he offered a HIGHER than market average commission. His way of thinking inspired me to rethink commissions altogether, to see if there was a different way which might better serve the homeowner.

Here is what I came up with:

UPSIDE DOWN commissions

It's been my experience that **most Realtors fight for their clients to get the best possible deal**; however, the statistics from the National Association of Realtors (NAR) suggest differently.

The book *Freakonomics* by Steven Levitt and Stephen Dubner point out with a solid argument that the most common commission structures do NOT incentify Realtors to dig and scrape for every possible dollar on behalf of the homeowner.

Instead, because the structure has the lion's share on the first $100,000.00, Realtors just tend to just get the deal DONE instead of done for the highest possible dollar amount. The solution to this seemed very simple to me... why not just turn the structure upside down?

Here is what UPSIDE DOWN commission looks like. Let's say we list your home for $500,000.00. If your listing commission is 7% of the first hundred thousand and 3% of the balance, the lion's share is paid regardless of the selling price.

Upside Down: 3% of the first $400,000.00 and 7% of the balance.

With Upside Down commissions:

1. You will keep more money in your pocket unless the home goes for full list price, in which case you will keep the exact same amount as the common structure.

2. Any amount under full list price, you will pay LESS than if you used the common commission structure.

3. You will have a better chance of your home selling for OVER list price, in which case you make even MORE money, regardless of shelling out more in commissions. Your NET profit is still higher than you were hoping for, as you were expecting the house to sell for under list price.

4. You KNOW that both the buyer's agent and your listing agent are incentified to get you every last nickel for your home. Even though the buyer's agent should really not be influenced by the commissions, the argument in *Freakonomics* is that they ARE influenced. This influence is not in the best interests of the buyers, but is favorable for the sellers.

5. In markets where 6% of the entire selling price is common, remember that you can always negotiate a different structure if you choose.

6. If you think about your home sale as a business transaction, you have to focus on your NET profit. This means the commissions are irrelevant as long as you keep as much money as possible in your hands. 100% of nothing is still nothing, so if you sell for OVER asking price, every dime is pure gravy for you. If you share a little bit of the gravy, there is still a lot left for you.

Freakonomics on YouTube: https://www.youtube.com/watch?v=17jO_w6f8Ck

The potential downside of Upside Down commissions is that the structure is unfamiliar to most Realtors and they may be inadvertently discouraged to show your home. If they mistakenly think the commission structure will result in a pay cut, they could potentially ignore your home.

One solution is to keep the commission which you offer to buyer's agents the same as what is common, then have upside down commissions only on the listing side of the commission structure. This still accomplishes much of what you are trying to achieve by being creative with the commission structure. You always have the option of inventing and proposing your own commission structure ideas to your Realtor to see what you come up with.

Whether you are selling on your own or with the service of a "by owner" company, you will want to put a lot of thought into how much to offer Realtors so they consider bringing their clients to you. The vast majority of home buyers use a Realtor, so if you don't engage the Realtor community, you are missing out on the majority of buyers.

If you offer ZERO or a relatively small fee, you will be missing out on the majority of potential buyers. If you are willing to offer a fee and your home is on the MLS system, ensure the amount is clearly posted so you ensure Realtors don't assume there isn't a fee offered.

If you are one of the people who absolutely loathes Realtors, you might wish to hold your nose just long enough so you can let one bring you a buyer.

Full service commissions

The truth is, Realtors have a LOT of annual expenses. My personal hard costs for various professional fees are around $20,000.00 per year. On top of this 20k, I also have to factor in all the other costs of running a business, which add up in a heck of a hurry.

The bottom line is that I have to sell a LOT of homes before I start seeing a reasonable net profit. Because of my expenses, I only give discounts in special circumstances. For instance, if I've done a few deals with you in the past or if you are a consistent source of referrals for me, I will make sure your contributions to my business are rewarded. If you have ZERO equity in your home, I may give you some free advice to help you sell on your own, and may even help you with the purchase contract. However, if we are only doing one deal together, I don't offer discounts on the promise of future support. Now, this is just how I personally have always run my business, and my practices are my own. When you're choosing a Realtor, each individual has their own set of personal rules they live and work by.

Section Notes

What was my greatest take-away from this section?

What do I need to remember about this section?

25

Disloyalty Can be Costly for Investors

Have you ever been cheated on? Most people will cringe at this question because the answer is usually "yes". However it happened, being cheated on hurts whether it's in business or in your personal life. The sense of betrayal takes the wind right out of your sails and leaves a lasting scar. You may forgive the person who betrayed you, but you will never forget, and the trust will never be what it once was between you.

Yes... trust must be earned. And yes, in most cases when your client leaves you, you can point the finger at yourself, but that is not always the case.

Realtors often meet potential clients who are looking for an investment property to either hold or flip. Often, the would-be investors are either new or relatively new to investing. If you have purchased less than ten investment properties within a five year period... you're still relatively new to the game. You'll be familiar with the game, but you're not an expert.

The pros have learned the hard way that playing the field with Realtors means they lose out on the best deals because when they pop up, the Realtor goes to his/her top three most loyal clients first with the opportunity. **It's human nature to reward loyalty with loyalty,** so when you tell a Realtor, "Hey, if you find a great deal, call me!" you won't be the first one called unless you have a solid relationship with your Realtor.

In the last few years, the game has changed with the types of relationships buyers and Realtors can solidify. You can sign agreements for a specific type of property in a specific area with one Realtor, and other areas / properties with other Realtors. This keeps everything above board, but the issue for the buyer is that each Realtor is working for a 50/50 chance of a pay-cheque. Imagine yourself putting in 40 hours of work for a 50/50 chance of a pay-cheque... How hard would you work? How committed would you be to your employer?

The bottom line is, pick a Realtor you trust and stick with them for as long as they are doing a good job. Anything less, and your Realtor will never bring you the best deals.

26

The Secret Truth About "Commission Free" For-Sale-By-Owner Companies and Discount Realtors

"A rose by any other name is still a rose, and fees by any other name are still fees."

Realtor fees are 100% negotiable, and the form of those fees are also 100% negotiable. Instead of commission, you may do a deal for either trade or a flat fee. For example, I once sold a home for a lawn tractor as payment. If you propose a fair deal which makes sense, I'll probably go for it.

Many "For Sale By Owner" (FSBO) companies offer great packages. Where I take exception is when they bend the truth by saying they are "commission free". **That's just not being honest.**

Most FSBO companies charge a "flat fee" for listing your home. This fee is non-refundable and non-negotiable. Also, you pay this fee regardless of whether or not your home actually sells. The **list-to-sale ratio** on FSBO companies is well below the national average for full-service, professional Realtors, yet they charge you upfront, regardless of the result. If your home doesn't sell, it is the seller who is out of pocket. FSBOs often don't sell and end up being listed by professional Realtors, leaving you out of pocket for the FSBO listing fees on top of Realtor fees. **The FSBO companies don't have any skin in the game. If your home doesn't sell, why would they care since they already have your money?**

The cost of marketing a home can vary greatly. The direct out-of-pocket investment many Realtors make to list and market your home can easily exceed $1,500.00, so once a Realtor has listed your home, they are VERY motivated to get it sold. If your home doesn't sell, the Realtor loses out on their investment of both time and money. Most Realtors only charge you if or when your home successfully sells. There are exceptions, but this is the norm. If your home does not sell, it's the Realtor, not the homeowner who is out of pocket.

If a homeowner changes their mind and decides to refuse an offer, they can often cancel their contract at no cost. The only exception is if an unconditional offer at full list price is made. In this rare circumstance, the Realtor fees become due; however, the homeowner still does not have to accept the offer.

Your actual cost of using a FSBO company is your non-refundable listing fee, plus the full market value commission you'll likely need to offer a buyer's agent. So, where are the savings?

Who are the most likely buyers you will most likely attract? The short answer is: "Predators"

Everyone wants to avoid paying more than they need to for any good or service. When you're car shopping, you check out all your options before you buy, and when you're home shopping you do the same.

Bargain hunting home buyers are always looking for foreclosures, highly motivated sellers, and unrepresented sellers. If you search FSBOs on Kijiji, you will see that half the ads are posted by professional home buyers who claim to be willing to pay "top dollar" for any home, in any condition. They actually claim that instead of "buy low, sell high", they are willing to "buy high". If this seems like an odd business model, it's because they are not being truthful. Professional home buyers are looking for unrepresented buyers who they can take advantage of.

Do you think this couldn't happen to you? If so, here is how smart people accept terrible deals.

The fact that you are selling without an experienced Realtor is the FIRST tool the bargain hunters try to use against you.

First, they ask to view your home then they sit down to make you an offer. The bargain hunter may sound something like this:

"Nice home you have here! It needs a lot of work, but it is really quite nice and I think it might work for us. You are asking $400,000.00 and you're not paying a Realtor, so really we can knock off $16,000.00, which puts us at $384,000.00... right? Oh, sorry, you paid $1,000.00 to a FSBO company, so lets make it an even $385,000.00. Does that sound about right? Yes? Okay, well, let's look at the SOLD properties in your area to check if you are asking a fair price.

At this point in the game, the bargain hunter will show you cherry picked properties which SOLD for far less than you are asking. It's easy to make properties which are inferior look like they are comparable; all you have to do is hide the data which makes them look bad and highlight the data which makes them look good.

"Well, it looks like we have a problem. It's normal for people to over-price their own home, but as you can clearly see, your home should only sell for roughly $375,000.00. Do you see what I mean? When you subtract the Realtor fees, the net to you would be about $350,000.00 if you were being

realistic. I'll tell you what I'm prepared to do. I'll help you out by paying $5,000.00 more than market value and I'll do a cash deal. I've prepared an offer for $355,000.00, and all you have to do is sign it, and your house is SOLD. You can even pick any possession date you wish, and I'll pay for your moving truck! You don't even have to clean up after yourself. Just move out and we will do all the after cleaning so you don't have to worry about a thing."

The bargain hunters know how to make this look like a good deal, and often people will go for it. Among the dangers of doing a deal like this is that most homeowners have no idea about the liabilities they may have just incurred. Bargain hunters want more than the best possible price, they also want to make sure that all the liability is on YOU, and not them. Without representation, you will not have a level playing field against the bargain hunter, and you could be on the hook for far more than you are aware.

Savvy buyers will talk you into carrying the mortgage for the first six months and make it sound like a great deal for you, when in fact, it's a terrible risk to take. If they fail to make a mortgage payment, you can be sure the contract does not have any liability for the buyers. The problem will fall on YOU to keep the mortgage payments current. Paying two mortgages is more than most people can handle, so you'll have to make darn sure the purchase contract has you covered.

But... you have a lawyer! If you've signed the unconditional contract and have received a deposit... it's too late. Your house is SOLD. The lawyer can't help you at this point of the transaction unless the contract is somehow non-binding.

"*I have this covered... my FSBO company has assigned me a Realtor, so this couldn't happen.*" Well...

The bargain hunters have thought of that one too, and know exactly how to work around this obstacle. They simply get you to show them the contract you have with the FSBO company, then write the relevant offer dates to fall outside of any obligation you may have to the FSBO company. Also, if you try to get advice from the FSBO "Realtor" who was assigned to you, just remember they are only getting paid a pittance and they have more than 100 other FSBO sellers who demand their time.

Who are the FSBO Realtors? I looked into one company who tried to recruit me and found out they pay a solid salary of $50,000.00/year to be an area manager. No Realtor can live off of $50,000.00 a year because our hard costs are easily around $20,000.00/year. Any Realtor who takes a position of area manager with a FSBO company is either retired or is part time. Either way, you're not going to get great representation.

FSBO Realtors are kind of like free public defenders. The best lawyers fetch top dollar, and the worst ones tend to be public defenders. The best Realtors all work for themselves, and they all earn a healthy income. You get what you pay for. If the FSBO Realtors could earn more, they would earn more.

Beware of "Bait and Switch" style tactics

Some discount Realtors offer the public great rates which are drastically lower than the competition. On the surface, the idea of super low commissions seems like a great deal; however, just like the FSBO companies, they don't mention what you should consider offering to the Realtor who brings you the buyer. If you offer drastically less than other home sellers, the Realtor could be strongly discouraged to bring a buyer to you.

*****DISCLAIMER*****

Each Real Estate Board has its own rules, and there are also national rules set out by CREA (The Canadian Real Estate Association). Further, there are also rules which are across North America which are set out by NAR. These rules are subject to change. The rules may or may not say that Realtors cannot discriminate against listed properties which offer low commissions. This rule can change at any time, and may vary in different selling areas.

What can happen is you meet the salesperson to talk about low listing fees, then they start telling you the REST of the upselling story.

- Yes, these are our low rates, but for these rates we have a limited "starter package"
- If you pay a little more, this is what we can add into the service package!
- And if you pay EVEN MORE, then THIS is what we can do for you!
- Oh, and I forgot to mention, if you really want to go for it, here is our "Professional Grade" package

Before you know it, you're paying just as much if not MORE than you would have with a full-time, full-service, professional Realtor. Also, many if not all of these fees may be up-front and non-refundable.

Keep in mind that **all commissions are negotiable**, for all licensed Realtors. Whatever the "discount people" are offering, any Realtor can technically match. That being said, just because someone CAN cut their rates, doesn't mean they will. For those who are quick to drop their rates for you, I suggest you ask them a few questions:

- Why did you buckle so easily?
- How easily will you buckle when negotiating on my behalf?
- Who else do you let steamroll you when the pressure is on?

- What kind of a negotiator do I want working for me when I'm buying a house or when I'm selling my own home?
- Where can I find a Realtor who is a strong negotiator and will be a strong advocate for me?
- Why do you feel that your services are worth so much less than other Realtors? Are they worth less?

Section Notes

What was my greatest take-away from this section?

What do I need to remember about this section?

27

Personal Safety and Security While Selling / Buying

Allow me to start with a true story which happened to a client and me:

I was setting up to host an open house for a new listing. Prior to leaving, the homeowner and I were having a chat at the entrance when we saw a vehicle pull up. A well dressed, large man stomped into the home, glanced around, looked at me and said in a gruff and aggressive tone, "Who are you"? I introduced myself then the man looked at the homeowner and asked him the same question. The homeowner identified himself, then our boisterous guest introduced himself as Bob, an important and successful Real Estate investor. The homeowner said, "Well, Bob, I'm just on my way out, but you can direct any of your questions to Mark, my Realtor." Bob snapped himself erect, planted his hands on his hips and retorted, "You will go nowhere! I will give you $350,000.00 for your home right now, and you must accept!"

The list price was $475,000.00, making Bob's offer ridiculous. The owner and I exchanged a nervous look of alarm, and I took control of the conversation from there. With a kind smile I looked at Bob and said, "Well, sir, that sounds wonderful, but in order to make an official offer, it has to be in writing. Why don't you meet me at my office in an hour. I'll shut down the open house and meet you there?" Bob glared at me and replied with a raised voice, "I am making an offer NOW! I will NOT meet you anywhere. You shut your mouth, I want to hear from the owner!" Big, angry Bob was out of control. The owner said to crazy Bob, "I need you to leave. Get out of my house." Bob went berserk. After a heated exchange and threats of beating us up, Bob the Berserker stormed out, yelling about how important he was, then roared away in his beat up old clunker of a car.

I immediately called my office to put out a group page to all of the other agents to beware of Bob the Berserker. Because of the violent actions of Bob, I also called the police to let them know what was going on. It was the craziest thing I've ever had happen to me at an open house, but it could have been a lot worse.

Realtor Lindsay Buziak was murdered in Saanich, British Columbia in 2008. She received a phone call from a stranger asking to view a vacant property which was listed at over one million dollars. Eager to get a new client, Lindsay met with the caller at the home. Lindsay was killed at the home, and her murder remains unsolved. You can visit https://lindsaybuziakmurder.com for full details of the murder and her father's continued search for justice.

Predators have also been known to pose as buyers in order to "case the joint". They will come in to assess whether or not it would be worth their while to break in later and rob you. Typically, Realtors know who their buyer clients are, and have collected a copy of their identification. This isn't always the case, however, as seen in the case of Lindsay Buziak. Realtors are often eager to meet with total strangers for the chance of securing a new client, but also have to take precautions when meeting strangers.

If you are selling your own home, always make sure you are not showing the house alone. At the very least, have a friend know there is a showing, and have them call you at a set time to check in on you.

You should at least know SOMETHING about the buyer ahead of time. If someone calls you on your cell and books an appointment to view your home, record the number on your phone and include it on your "showing log". Keep a log of every showing and include as much information as you can. If someone knocks on your door without an appointment and you decide to let them in, at least get their licence plate number and take note of the make and model of their vehicle for your showing log.

Many security systems have doorbell cameras now. If you have this type of system, make sure your settings are set to capture images of everyone who is coming and going. **Make sure you point out this security feature to the potential buyer and tell them the images are stored in the "cloud", whether they are or not.** I'm an honest person, but this is one situation where I suggest fibbing if the images are not actually stored on the cloud.

Another useful "fib" if you're showing the home alone is to say something like, "We will have to make this quick because my friend "BIG EDDY" will be here any minute. He's always coming over to check on me, he's just so darn protective. He's scary looking, but he's really just a gentle giant... as long as he doesn't lose his temper, that is. You don't want to be around when he loses that temper of his! But he's working on that. Really though, he's a great guy."

Or "I have to ask, we have seven hidden cameras in the house... did you notice any of them? We plan to leave them with the house. Aren't they hidden well?"

Your belongings can be replaced, but your life can't. It's easy to be lackadaisical in your security measures, but it only takes one bad event to make you regret not taking preventative measures to protect yourself.

Section Notes

What was my greatest take-away from this section?

What do I need to remember about this section?

28

Rent To Own Myths and Misconceptions

by Shawna Roch

A **Rent To Own** (RTO) program can create a great opportunity for **tenant buyers** to buy their dream home. A Tenant Buyer is a tenant with an interest in their residence, who intends to transition towards freehold ownership of their residence.

For people who have been turned down by traditional lending, an RTO program could serve as a viable option whether you have been through a bankruptcy, facing foreclosure, gone through a divorce, or are self employed.
There are a lot of misconceptions out there on Rent to Own. In part, this is because there are so many ways to structure a Rent to Own. If you structure the RTO properly, it becomes a win-win scenario for both the tenant buyer and the investor. In some cases, a win-win-win as there could be:

- A tenant buyer
- Investor managing the deal
- A money partner brought in

Some investors focus on the property first; however, to end up with your ideal win-win scenario, the tenant buyer should be able to choose their own property. When they choose their own property, they are both more excited about the home and more committed to transitioning into ownership.

Some myths are:

– If you don't work on repairing your credit, you will definitely lose your deposit

It depends. The whole idea is to work towards owning your own home and repairing any credit issues that are of concern to lending institutions. If you do not repair your credit, at the end of the term it would be up to the investor to renegotiate terms to give you an extension that would be required to repair your credit. Let's face it, life sometimes gets in the way and we all need a little help.

– All rent is applied to your down payment

This would be nice... but no. The rent is calculated at a fair market rent value. Depending on the amount you have to put down in the beginning, you will need to come up with the difference for your down payment to the bank. This amount is divided up by the number of months in the term and it then becomes your monthly option consideration. You can think of it as a forced savings plan.

– You don't get to choose your own home

This depends on the investor you choose to work with for your Rent to Own. Some investors focus on properties first, others focus on tenants first. It's in the investor's best interest to help you move into a home that you actually want to be in. When you love your home, you tend to do a better job of taking care of it and are more motivated to transition into ownership.

Beware of predatory lending

Sadly, there are people who prey on those who are about to lose their homes. They come in and offer a price which is way under fair market value, and justify it with a slick sales pitch. Then they have the tenant buyers commit to a Rent to Own contract, knowing full well the homeowners are very likely to default. Once the homeowners have defaulted on the RTO contract, they are evicted and the investor then sells the home at a profit.

Protect yourself

You can lose your life's savings on an RTO if you trust the wrong people. Unfortunately, there are bad people out there in the world who do bad things. Whether you're a tenant buyer looking for your forever home or a joint venture partner wanting to make a greater-than-average return on your investment, you have to be very careful about who you do business with.

Usually a tenant buyer is someone who was turned down by the bank because their credit score was too low. This can be because of:

- High TDSR (Total Debt Service Ratio)
- Less than perfect credit history
- No credit history at all
- Previous bankruptcy
- Unstable work history
- Unstable residence history
- Recent change in profession / trade
- Self employment
- Unrecognized combined income (new life partner)

They may be forced to wait for years before they can qualify according to the bank, so out of desperation they respond to an RTO ad on kijiji and meet with a guy or gal. Before they know it, they give $10,000.00 (their life's savings) to this person and Voila, they are in a Rent to Own program. Meanwhile, they are struggling with paying their credits cards and rent. After a few months go by, they default on the rent and are evicted, losing their deposit and all their savings. It's a scenario that happens all too often and one which crooked investors hope for.

What to look for in a properly structured Rent to Own Program:

What we all want is a win-win scenario. Here is an overview of a professional Rent to Own flow:

– Tenant Buyer contacts a Rent to Own expert.

- Interview the expert; ask them for their educational background, industry references, and make sure they understand what they are doing and can fully explain how a Rent to Own works. Even if you don't fully understand it yourself, the person you are talking to should be able to sit down and go over a step-by-step process that makes perfect sense.
- As the Tenant Buyer, you will be asked to fill out a Client Questionnaire and a Rental Application. All of this will be reviewed in person and a monthly budget will be discussed. An initial option consideration will be determined, and at this point you either commit to the program or not.

PRO TIP: Seek your own independent legal council.
From there, the Investor will bring in their credit team consisting of a professional Mortgage Broker and a Credit Repair Specialist. This is the critical point at which you are either a go to proceed or you stop to discuss why a Rent to Own may not be a fit for you at this time. In the example above where the tenant buyer lost their $10,000.00 in savings, this would have been discovered through proper due diligence, and no harm would have been done.

- If you are good to go with the Mortgage Broker and the Credit Repair Specialist, there will be a predetermined amount which you qualify for at the end of your term. However, keep in mind there are steps you will need to take in order to get there. This is where the Credit Repair

Specialist comes in. They will put together a tailored three year plan for your specific situation. A good Credit Repair Specialist will check in with you either quarterly or biannually to make sure you are on track.

- For the next phase, you would meet with a Realtor, make a wish list and start looking for your forever home. The Realtor will be an integral part of your Rent to Own Investor's team of professionals. Once the property is approved by both you and the investor, then an offer is made. If the offer is accepted and conditions are met, "Yay!" you now have your forever home.

- The lease agreement and option to purchase contracts are prepared, all parties sign the contracts, and the tenant buyer moves in and celebrates.

There are many ways to structure a Rent to Own, and they are not all created equal. This is an advanced Real Estate investing strategy and should only be engaged in by educated professionals.

I am known to turn down a potential tenant buyer for their own good. In one case, during my due diligence process, we met to go over their financial situation and discovered that they had less than half of what we would normally require as a down payment. Also, they could not afford any monthly option consideration payments which would go towards their down payment at the end of the term when they would choose to exercise their option to purchase. During this conservation, the potential tenant buyers were open and honest about their situation and we all agreed they should stay where they were renting for another year and save up some money.

Honest investors are willing to tell you NO. Predatory investors will encourage you to go forward, regardless of your situation. Don't be overly eager to do a deal. If the numbers don't work, then just walk away.

Another past client of mine passed the first screening test, went through the mortgage broker process, and set up a three year payment schedule to pay down their credit cards; it was all looking good. We determined a purchase price that they could qualify for at the end of a three year term, and we were off and running with the Realtor to look for houses. Unfortunately, we hit a wall as the tenant buyers wanted to buy in an area that was out of their price range. It was hard for them to understand that even if they could qualify for the house three years later, the fair market rent was still out of their price range. They wanted to drink champagne but only had a beer budget. This would have been far too risky for us, as it was highly likely they would not be able to afford the property at the end of the term. More importantly, it was far too risky for THEM. Had we allowed them to get in over their heads, the chances of default would have been significant.

An Investor's point of view

There are investors who do the complete Rent to Own on their own, qualify for the mortgage and have the money down. But let's face it, in today's market with the lending rules constantly changing, you can only qualify for so many mortgages on your own. If you are building a portfolio, at some point you are going to need both money and credit partners.

Have your investor manage the deal with all its moving parts. Let your investor work with the team of professionals to make sure all the due diligence is completed. Never take shortcuts on home inspections or insurance, etc. Shortcuts can come and bite you in the butt. Take the time, spend the money and do it right.

Typically, if you have done your due diligence and are working with a professional mortgage broker to qualify your tenant buyers, you can make an educated decision whether or not to move forward with this tenant. Your ideal Tenant Buyer needs to be both fully qualified and have skin in the game. Otherwise, what is stopping them from walking away, trashing your property, or both?

RTO is not a buy-rent-hold strategy. The objective of an RTO is to buy the house for the purpose of renting for a term, with the option to purchase at the end. You are looking for responsible, employed people who are having a temporary setback on their credit. These people typically want to own their own home so bad but need two to four years to make that happen. This ideal tenant buyer would have a combined household income of at least $110,000. Ideal tenants are excited and grateful to you for helping make their dreams come true. This is a "feel-good" strategy when done the right way.

RTO is an advanced strategy with several moving parts. If you're considering selling your primary residence using an RTO strategy, team up with an investor who is an expert in Rent to Owns. They can buy your home from you and save you a lot of grief in the long run.

Section Notes

What was my greatest take-away from this section?

What do I need to remember about this section?

29

Digging Yourself Out of the Rental Rut

If you are currently renting but would prefer to be an owner, it can be a frustrating position to be in. RTO (Rent To Own) is one potential strategy but it isn't the only one. Here are some other potential options.

1. Sublet, and save the rental revenue

When most people decide to sublet a part of their residence, they do so to reduce their rental burden. It's a smart move, but what's even smarter is to sublet and save all the revenue from your sub-tenants. Saving is not easy, but it is smart. Whether you are subletting a bedroom or an entire portion of the house, the revenue you save will add up very quickly.

Not all landlords allow you to sublet, and those who do may require you to have your sub-tenants fill out separate rental agreements. Whatever you do, make sure you have the permission of the landlord in writing before you sub-let. If you don't, you could risk getting yourself evicted.

The best place to put the revenue you save is into a Registered Retirement Savings Plan (RRSP). There are often programs where you can roll your RRSP into a down payment on a home without paying a penalty for using the RRSP. Programs are always changing, so be sure to ask your mortgage broker if there is a program available for you to capitalize on this valuable tool. You can also speak with a Certified Financial Planner to strategize the best way to squirrel away your money for a future down payment on a home. A good CFP can customize a program which fits your situation.

2. Live far below your means and save the balance

When my first marriage ended, I had to get creative in order to pay my ex-wife's rent. The only way I could afford to cover her rent was to not have to pay rent myself, which is a significantly challenging problem to solve. After much thought and exploration, I found an opportunity to be a "live in" respite worker for two intellectually challenged men. In exchange for helping to look after these two men, I was provided with a rent-free room. I stayed in that house for three wonderful years, and those two men became like family. This was a win-win situation for me as I loved respite work, and I was also able to provide for my children at the same time.

However you reduce your living expenses, it will likely require some short term sacrifice in order to meet your long term goals. If you are determined to own your own home, you just have to do what it takes in order to save up your down payment. Short term pain for long term gain. If you're concerned about your financial future, owning a home is one of the key ways to build wealth.

3. Joint Venture (JV)

There are many real estate investors who may be willing to JV with you in order for you to build your down payment.

Scenario #1:
An investor buys a fixer-upper and you provide the labour for all the renovations. Once the renovations are complete, the investor sells the property and splits the profits with you. Repeat this scenario once or twice and you will have enough for a down payment.

Scenario #2:
An investor buys a fixer-upper and you move in as a tenant. Over the course of an agreed upon period of time, you provide all the renovations. Once the renovations are complete, the investor sells the property and splits the profits with you. Repeat this scenario once or twice and you will have enough for a down payment.

Scenario #3:
An investor co-signs for you, but you provide the down payment for the mortgage. Once the renovations are

complete, you sell the property and share the profit with the investor at an agreed upon ratio or for an agreed upon fee. This is one of the better scenarios because the property becomes your primary residence, meaning you may be able to avoid paying capital gains taxes. Be sure to consult a chartered accountant before you spend your profits. The rules constantly change, so it is best not to assume.

Whichever scenario you choose, make sure you do NOT engage in the relationship without a clear contract which has been approved by your lawyer. Both you and the investor should have your own lawyers so you are both protected. Using the same lawyer can sometimes be problematic.

Section Notes

What was my greatest take-away from this section?

What do I need to remember about this section?

30

Buying or Selling a Condominium Property in Alberta

by Bernice (Bernie) Winter, ACCI, FCCI.
Founder of Condo-Check
www.condo-check.com

Buying a condominium is a common choice for people who are either downsizing or entering the real estate market. In either case, whether a first-time buyer or a retiree, the impact of a cash call levy can result in great financial and emotional stress. My hope in these few pages is to share some tips and insights to help you select the best condominium property for your needs.

Condominium living can be a wonderful experience when you select a project that compliments both your lifestyle and your financial means.

Some of the benefits of condominium ownership include:

- The shared cost to maintain the physical property
- The provision of services
- A Board of Directors (BOD or BoD)
- Property Management to administer the work required in the condominium project

Purchasing a Condominium is one of the largest financial investments most people will ever make. The ROI (Return On Investment) is realized when you sell the unit and cash in on the accumulated equity. It is therefore important to pay attention and be up-to-date on the management of the condominium operations that impact the saleability of your home. A well-managed unit will sell for the best dollar compared to the competition. When selling a condominium, it is important to know the status of the operations and have a complete package of documents to support the facts.

Factors on getting the best return for your investment

If you desire for a return on your investment and you want to enjoy the freedom to live in a well-maintained and managed property, then condominium ownership requires you to be a responsible owner. Being a responsible owner means you live in compliance with the rules, regulations and bylaws. It also requires you to read the information provided from time-to-time such as a newsletter, the annual budget, notices, etc. The following list identifies information, facts, and ways to be involved and protect your investment:

- Owners collectively elect the Board of Directors who are made up of fellow owners who volunteer to oversee the operations of the condominium
- Volunteering to be a board member is something every owner should consider doing as it gives you insight into the complexity of operating a project
- Attending the Annual General Meeting (AGM) is an opportunity to ask questions, meet the board and the property managers, and to learn how your investment in the project is being cared for
- Attend any extraordinary General Meetings
- Annually, owners are provided with documents such as the year-end operating budget so be sure to review these as soon as they're provided
- Review the corporate insurance policy and ensure you are aware of the deductibles and the insurance you will require (more on this later)
- Keep the documents you receive available for when you sell your condominium
- Report concerns to the property manager or appointed contact immediately: water escaping, unsavory characters hanging about, vehicle break-ins, items that don't belong in areas, etc.
- Review the five year Reserve Fund Plan
- Ask questions respectfully in writing and allow appropriate time to get a response; you don't know what the business of the day is when you send your question
- When a special assessment is levied (a cash call), the board is required to comply with the requirements of

the *Condominium Property Amendment Act 2014*, which requires the following to be provided to each owner before collecting any funds for a special levy:

- A notice detailing the purpose and amount of the levy
- Details on the amount of the levy each individual unit owner is responsible for and verification that it was charged based on the appropriate allocation method
- Schedule of when the payment is due
- Copy of the board meeting minutes showing the vote in favor of the levy
- Verification that the funds will be used for the purpose it was called for
- Verification that any surplus funds will be added to the reserve fund account

"Condominium" is a form or ownership, not a style of home. Though normally associated with attached housing, detached homes and even acreages can be condominiums. Which style of condo would you invest in for both comfort and peace of mind? The condition of the project does matter to the value of the property, and often can only be identified by reviewing the operations of a condominium.

Financial management factors

There are many factors that impact the costs of condominium ownership. Factors range from the number of owners sharing the costs to the size, condition and style of project. For example, a townhouse-style condominium will typically have lower condominium fees in comparison to a unit in an apartment building. Apartment buildings with elevators and underground parking will generally have higher expenses than an apartment which has no elevator and only exterior parking. Projects that offer amenities such as gyms, pools, social rooms, golf club memberships, tennis courts, concierge services, on-site security, full-service yard and building maintenance, etc. share in higher operating costs, which in the end are shared by the owners of the units via the condominium fees. These factors are important for you to consider as a buyer. Ask yourself which services and amenities are important to you.

The following list will assist you in this process:

- Lawn maintenance and snow removal provided by the condominium; townhome-style condominiums may require the individual owners to remove the snow and maintain the lawns and flowerbeds in the unit so be sure to verify what you prefer as this will impact the available projects which you can choose from
- Exterior window washing paid for by the condominium; again, townhome condos often make the cleaning of the windows an owner's responsibility
- Maintenance and replacement of the exterior building components provided by the condominium; some bare land condominiums require the owners to fully insure and maintain the buildings located within their units

- The corporation is responsible for replacement of exterior windows and doors; again, townhome condos often make the replacement of the windows an owner's responsibility (more on this later)
- Exercise room / gym with equipment
- Social room with equipment and furnishing such as a big screen TV, pool, foosball and other game tables, fireplace and common areas, etc.
- Tennis courts, equestrian trails, BBQ areas, etc.
- Indoor swimming pool
- Outdoor swimming pool
- Access to a golf course or club

One of the items overlooked in establishing the cost to operate, administer and manage the condominium project is the level of services expected by the owners collectively. For example, if the majority of owners want the snow removed from the parking before they leave for work each day or to have the snow hauled away and not piled up on site, there would most likely be additional costs, especially when it comes to hauling the snow away or having a priority status with the snow removal provider. These examples would substantially increase the annual cost for snow removal.

Owner responsibility when owning a condominium property in Alberta

Too often, condominium living is represented as carefree without mentioning the responsibilities that come with this carefree lifestyle. Carefree living can be a reality as the Board of Directors elected by the owners are responsible for the decisions made while governing the business of the condominium. They become the stewards of the condo's financial health and maintainers of the property condition. In addition, they procure and manage services such as snow removal and the cleaning of common areas. Each of these actions or inactions impact property value when it comes to the day you want to sell your unit.

As an owner, it is your responsibility to support the Board of Directors when they request input from owners, and to attend general or special meetings when called. These meetings are one of the communication streams available to owners. Many owners ask that the board mail or deliver documents on a regular basis; however, this can have a big impact on operating costs. This is the reason there are charges for document requests.

Know which items you are personally responsible for maintaining and/or replacing. Bylaw sections relating to "Duties of the Owners" and "Use and Occupancy" will provide this detail.

This can include:

- Exterior windows and doors
- Zone valves, thermostats, mechanical and heating systems within the unit
- Replacing light bulbs on balconies and patios

- Clearing snow on doorsteps and decks
- Weeding flower beds
- Yard maintenance

For some bare land condominiums, this can include all buildings, structures and landscaping within the boundary of the unit.

Being an active and invested owner can reduce operating costs and enhance the living quality.

These actions can include:

- Booking the elevator to move furnishings in or out
- Picking up flyers and papers that miss the bin in the lobby
- Respecting the use of the recycling and garbage areas
- Respect visitor parking rules
- Keep balconies, patios, decks, and yard clean and tidy
- Respect rules for pets on common property
- Follow the rules regarding storage on common property
- Read and respect the bylaws sections relating to "Duties of the Owners" and "Use and Occupancy".
- Within the unit, it is important to remember that the appliances, plumbing and electrical systems inside the unit are your responsibility to repair and maintain.
    - Items such as running toilets, dripping shower heads or taps can be signs of plumbing needs

    - ❍ Replace any hoses for water for fridges or washing machines with the braided versions instead of rubber as they don't tend to break or leak as often as the rubber version
- Immediately report any changes or noises that are new from zone valves or plumbing to the contact person provided
- Security – most important – DO NOT let anyone you do not know access the building or property
    - ❍ Remember that when you let someone into a secured apartment community, you are allowing them access to every home
    - ❍ Make it a practice to wait for the garage door to close when accessing or exiting the parking garage – don't let cars follow you in
- Contact the police for suspicious behavior and the fire department for fire or odours such as a potential gas leak

Insurance for the corporation and the unit

The Board of Directors has the responsibility of having insurance that covers the perils required in Section 47 of the *Condominium Property Act, RSA 2000 of Alberta*, Section 61 of the *Regulation to the Condominium Property Act*, in addition to any areas that the Corporation's registered Bylaws require.

Legislation requires the common property and personal property of the corporation be insured, plus any area(s) or capital components that the Bylaws require to have coverage. The bylaws and the items covered vary based on the type of condominium plan registered. Some bylaws require the condominium corporation insurance to cover "Improvements and Betterments" to the units while others do not. The items covered by the corporation insurance can vary from including windows and doors to zone valves, thermostats, and "Improvements and Betterments". It is important that the bylaws are being complied with when the condominium corporation is placing insurance, as much as it is for the individual owner who is required to carry, at minimum, insurance coverage for their contents and liability. Any item not covered by the corporation becomes the responsibility of the individual owners to include in their policies.

It is important to obtain a copy of the "Insurance Certificate" for the condominium so you can provide this and a copy of the Bylaws to your insurance company when placing coverage for condominium property. You can obtain a copy of the insurance policy from the Property Manager. The Condominium Property Act allows the Corporation ten days to provide a copy of the insurance policy once requested in writing.

Also, when you are seeking insurance, you can also ask about coverage for things like sewer backup, coverage for temporary accommodation if your home is severely damaged, etc.

Bylaws require that occupants and guests not do things that could cause risk or damage to people or property.

Note: Many bylaws state that if a claim is made under the Corporation policy due to an event that originates in a unit and the Board determines that its cause was the result of lack of care, or an act or omission of the owner or occupant, then that owner may be responsible for the corporation deductible for the claim. If the amount is less than the deductible, the cost of repairing the damage to all units and common area impacted may be required.

Condominium manager and the board

The relationship of the condominium property manager and the condominium Board of Directors is created by entering into a contract. This contract typically contains terms for annual renewal unless otherwise notified.

The Board of Directors is made up of owners who volunteer their time to oversee the operation of the condominium. The Board is responsible for using the best effort when overseeing the governance of the condominium. Examples of the responsibilities include (but are not limited to): annual budget approval, invoices paid, contractors selected, services provided, special assessments levied, bylaw infractions fined, insurance provider selected, operating in compliance with the reserve fund study and plan, and bylaws and the condominium legislation. It is mandatory for the Board to have Directors & Officers coverage in the corporate insurance policy as protection for the board members in case an honest error occurs.

The condominium manager is the administrative arm that supports the Board by monitoring the operations and guiding the Board accordingly. The manager is the contact person for the owners, contractors, buyers, etc. The condominium manager holds the records of the corporation, tracks the financial process (produces monthly financial statements for board approval), prepares the budgets, tenders for bids, and updates the Board on changes in the legislation.

Team for buying or selling a condominium unit

Whether you are buying or selling a condominium, the experience of the team you select is important. Be sure to hire team members that have condominium experience of at least ten years. The team includes the Lawyer, Realtor and Document Reviewer. The condominium is a specialty of its own in an ever-changing industry.

Have your condominium documents ready when you list a unit, and update yourself on the business of the condominium. The information provided will enable you to be prepared to establish your asking price in compliance with the evidence of either great management or poor management. If you know you do not have a well-managed condominium, you should not be surprised when a buyer asks for a reduction due to the condition of the operations.

Having a document review before listing a condominium can give you insight into how your condominium investment is being managed and provides you time to address any concerns before listing the unit.

Notes to condo living

(terms, definitions and general information)

Annual General Meeting (AGM)

The Condominium Property Act requires notice of a General Meeting to be provided to the owners, mortgagors and anyone who has notified the corporation of their interest in the unit, at least 14 days before the date of the meeting. The information in the notice is to include: date, hour, location of the meeting, notice of any special business to be addressed, and an agenda for the meeting.

The Annual General Meeting (AGM) is the one time of the year that owners are brought up-to-date with the business of the corporation. It is also the time when owners direct who they want making the business decisions for the corporation during the next year by electing the Board of Directors. The BOD for a condominium has a lot of power. Refer to Bylaw "Duties of the Corporation" and Bylaw "Powers of the Corporation". The owners elect this Board of Directors at the AGM. In Alberta, the legal system and the Condominium Property Act, RSA 2000 support reasonable decisions made by the Board. If you are unable to attend this important AGM, you can give your proxy to another person who will vote on your behalf at the meeting.

Annual operating budget

The annual operating budget is prepared and approved by the Board before each fiscal year end and is subject to changes adopted by the Board throughout the year. This budget is an estimate of the anticipated income required to operate for the upcoming fiscal year, based on the estimated expenses. If a shortfall should occur, the amount of contribution the owners make may change at any time during the year.

In a condominium, each owner is required to contribute an amount towards the maintenance of their investment in the condominium. This contribution is referred to as a "condominium fee". The individual owner's contribution is determined based on the Unit Factor allotted to the unit unless the Bylaws provide an alternate formula. The contributions are collected then used to provide the services (snow removal, landscaping), building maintenance and operating costs, repairs, Common Property utilities, insurance, etc. Refer to the items listed in the operating budget for complete details.

It is typical in an apartment-style unit that heat, water and sewer for the units are included in the common expenses.

However, we suggest that you confirm this is the case. Power in a condominium budget is typically for the common area only. Be sure to transfer the utilities that apply. For a townhome-style unit, typically the power and gas (heat) is the owner's responsibility.

In addition to these costs, the Condominium Corporation is mandated by law to have a reasonable reserve fund in place for the replacement and repair of major capital items.
The operating budget includes funds to pay for the cost of operating the Managed Property and the Common Property elements, and any area in the unit that the Bylaws make the responsibility of the corporation.

Bylaws

The Bylaws for the corporation are given power by the Condominium Property Act, RSA 2000 of Alberta. Any bylaw registered with the corporation is enforceable as law. It is important that the registered Bylaws are customized to suit the needs of the individual site. To obtain a registered copy of the Bylaws, visit the Alberta Land Titles Office or order them online (follow the link on our website www.condo-check.com). Registered Bylaws apply to all occupants of the units (owners and tenants).

It is advisable that as a purchaser you read the following sections of bylaws to ensure that you are aware of ALL your obligations as an owner. It is important to note that the names of these headings may vary as the writers of bylaws often choose to be unique. Be open-minded and a bit creative as you search for the following topics: Table of Contents; Definitions and Interpretations; Duties of the Owners; Owner's Obligation to Repair and Maintain; and Use and Occupancy Restrictions. If you are a board member, the remaining sections of the Bylaws apply to the managing and operating of the Condominium Corporation.

The corporation's registered Bylaws outline the corporation's responsibilities and powers. The Bylaws determine the duties of the Board of Directors and the responsibilities and restrictions of the owners.

The fining sections of the Condominium Property Act of Alberta are only available to a condominium if they are included in their Bylaws. Note: If the registered Bylaws for a condominium does not specifically provide for fines for breach of the bylaw, it is recommended that the bylaws be amended, as the only remedy available when bylaws do not provide for fining is to take the owner to court. If the Bylaws do not provide a method for collecting condominium contributions (fees), all fees and special assessments (cash calls) are to be collected based on each Owner's Unit Factor.

In regards to fees and assessments, the Condominium Property Act, RSA 2000 gives the corporation the power to foreclose for unpaid fees and assessments. Be aware that every Board of Directors has the authority to special assesses without consulting all the owners. Bylaws give them the authority to obtain funds in the case of an emergency, a budget shortfall or for financial needs that are more than the current contributions by way of Special Assessment.

NOTE: If the Condominium Bylaws conflict with the Condominium Property Act, the Condominium Act will prevail over the conflicting Bylaws

---

Condominium legislation

Currently, there are three components to the condominium legislation in Alberta. This legislation is in the process of being amended. More amendments are expected over the next few years, so check the Service Alberta website for updates. As of May 2018, the following are the governing documents:

"2014 Act" means the Condominium Property Amendment Act, 2014, Statues of Alberta 2014, Chapter 10

"Act" means the *CONDOMINIUM PROPERTY ACT*, Revised Statutes of Alberta, 2000, Chapter C□22, as amended from time to time, or any statute or statutes passed in

"Board" means the Board of Directors of the Corporation

"Regulation" or "Regulations" means the *Condominium Property Act* Regulation, currently being Alberta Regulation 168/2000 and any other Regulation made from time to time in substitution, replacement or addition thereto by the Lieutenant Governor in Council in Alberta pursuant to the Act.

Condominium plan and unit factor

The registered Condominium Plan identifies the legal boundaries of the unit, the description of the common property and any exclusive use areas. Refer to the surveyor's notes on the first page of the condominium plan for specific information on things such as determining the location of the boundaries between the unit and the common property.

The boundaries of the unit determine the areas of ownership (the separation between what is owned under the title and what is shared as "Common Property"). Common Property is owned collectively by all the owners in the complex. Defining the boundaries between the units and the common property helps establish the different responsibilities of the owners and the corporation.

Unit Factors and the unit size in square meters are designated on the Condominium Plan. A Condominium Corporation is based on a total of 10,000 Unit Factors. The unit factor assigned to the individual unit represents the owner's undivided interest share (ownership) of the

Common Property of the Condominium Corporation. The unit factor determines the owner's voting rights, as well as the portion of the operating budget or any special assessment owners are required to contribute unless the Bylaws state otherwise. In Alberta, the registered Bylaws may state a method of determining the amount of the contribution based on a formula other than the unit factors.

Condominium sheet or CAD

The Condominium Additional Plan Sheet (also referred to as a CADS or CS) contains any registrations against the Condominium Plan such as: charges against the corporation; caveats; easements; re-division of units; the registration date for the Bylaws; amendments to the plan; resolution for windows and doors, and change of the Board of Directors. Information can be registered on this document through the South Alberta Land Titles Office.

The owners of each residential unit shall have the right to the exclusive use of any portions of the common property that may be designated by the corporation (typically the storage lockers, balconies, yard areas and parking stalls).

Estoppel Certificate

The Estoppel Certificate is a legal document that certifies what amounts or charges affect the unit, as well as any anticipated charges against the unit. The Estoppel Certificate, at the date of issue, terminates any obligation of the issuing owner for debt or charges to the referenced unit.

The lawyer for the purchaser requests the Estoppel Certificate at the time the title is transferred. Request that your lawyer provides you with a copy of the Certificate clear of all charges.

Exclusive use and privacy areas

Any such Exclusive Use privacy area shall be maintained and kept tidy at the sole expense of the owner. If an owner fails to properly maintain any exclusive use area after a notice has been given by the Board, the Board can order the maintenance corrected then charge back the costs to the owner.

Bylaws often restrict things like storage of combustibles, use of BBQs, flags, storage sheds and bicycle storage, and can restrict things like (but not limited to) the planting of flowers, shrubs and trees. Refer to the sections of your Bylaws regarding "Use and Occupancy Restrictions," "Privacy and Parking," and "Exclusive Use Areas."

Parking – assigned or leased

Parking stalls that are Exclusive Use Common Property are allotted to the owners by either assignment or using a Lease Agreement. If no lease agreement is provided with the documents, the common property parking stalls are assigned to each owner by the Board of Directors. The assignments can change at the discretion of the Board.

Parking areas, whether leased or assigned, are common property areas that the individual owners have exclusive right to use; however, in most cases, the repair and maintenance of these areas are the responsibility of the Board of Directors, except as defined in the Bylaws. Owners will most likely *not be allowed* to store items or allow oil to leak on the parking surface, and owners are responsible for keeping these areas clean and tidy.

Reserve Fund Study and Reserve Fund Plan

The reserve account is a fund established for the replacement of capital items on the common property.

A Reserve Fund Study gives the Board of Directors a guideline to follow which will minimize the risk of future special assessments to repair or replace capital items such as the roof, building envelope (the physical separator between the conditioned and unconditioned environment of a building, including the resistance to air, water, heat, light and noise transfer), fencing, roadways, parking areas, etc. The Reserve Study and Plan will list the items that this fund applies to. A Reserve Fund Study customizes the corporation's financial projections to meet the needs of the individual site. It is prudent for an owner or a buyer to read the Reserve Fund Report provided so they are aware of the information provided by the inspector.

The Board of Directors has the power to adopt and operate based on a Reserve Fund Plan that they have adopted. This plan is required to be based on the Study and Report provided. However, the Board, at their discretion, may make adjustments to the Reserve Fund Plan. By reviewing the report, owners will be aware of any adjustments made by the Board.

Once a Corporation has completed its Reserve Fund Study and Plan, the Act requires the same process to be taken every five years (i.e. new Reserve Fund Study & Plan).

NOTE: If a Reserve Fund Study has not yet been completed for a condominium, persons buying and selling units in the complex may experience difficulties obtaining a mortgage from their bank and may find their lawyer refusing to conclude the deal.

Rental of a condominium unit

If an owner desires to lease or rent his unit, the *Condominium Property Act of Alberta* provides that the owner shall:

- Not be restricted from doing so
- Must inform the corporation of their intent to rent or lease the unit

- Inform the tenant or lessee that they will be required to comply with the provisions of the Act and the Bylaws of the Corporation
- Not be released of any of his obligations and shall be jointly and severally liable with the proposed lessee or occupant concerning such obligations
- Understand that the corporation may require a deposit for wear and tear on common property; the deposit cannot exceed one month's rent
- Understand that should the owner miss paying a monthly condominium fee, the corporation has the right to collect the rent and deduct the amount owed
- Understand that if a tenant breaches a bylaw, the tenant and the owner may be fined equally
- Understand that the corporation has the power to order the eviction of the tenant if the tenant is consistently in breach of the Bylaws; should this occur, the owner is required to evict the tenant following the notice period required under the *Residential Tenancy Act*

Special Assessment Levy

If at any time it appears that the annual contributions towards the common expenses will be insufficient to meet the common expenses, the corporation may assess and collect a special contribution or assessment against each unit in an amount sufficient to cover the additional anticipated common expenses. The corporation will give notice of such further assessment to all owners, which will include a written statement setting out the reasons for the assessment, and each assessment will be due and payable by each owner in the manner and on the date or dates specified in the notice. Each special assessment will be determined and assessed against the owners in proportion to their unit factors or by the Bylaws.

The Bylaws often state that all such special assessments are to be payable within ten days of the due date for payment as specified in the notice, and if not paid, will bear interest until paid.

Special Resolution

A resolution passed at a meeting of the corporation where at least fourteen days' notice specifying the proposed resolution has been given, by

a. A majority of not less than seventy-five percent of all the units vote, either personally or by proxy, in favor of the resolution

b. The number of unit factors represented by the votes cast in favour of the resolution is at least seventy-five percent of the unit factors for all the units

The procedures for voting on a special resolution where a unit is owned by two or more persons must be in accordance with the regulations. A vote under this section must be signed by the person voting.

The results of a vote on special resolution must be recorded in the minutes of the general
meeting at which the vote was conducted:

a. The number of votes in respect of units and unit factors in favour of the resolution
b. The number of votes in respect of the unit factors of the resolution

Notice and requirements for written votes

a. The notice is to contain the date in which the vote is to be received by the board, along with any other prescribed information
b. The date which the votes must be received must be no later than one year from the date the notice of the proposed resolution was sent
c. The date by which the votes must be calculated must be no later than 14 days from the date referred to in the original notice
d. A vote must be signed by the person voting
e. The records must include the number of votes in respect to the units and unit factors in favour of the resolution
f. The number of votes in respect to the units and unit factors not in favour of the resolution

g. Results must be provided to the owners who have given a written request

Retention of voting records

The Board must retain the original votes cast by qualified persons by the regulations.

Section Notes

What was my greatest take-away from this section?

What do I need to remember about this section?

31

Water Wells

by Troy Niemans

The chances are that if you own a rural property, you also own both a water well and a septic system (which we will discuss later). Whether you are a seasoned rural resident or you are new to rural life, this section can save you a lot time, money and hassle.

The biggest and most crucial differences between rural and urban properties are where they get their drinking water FROM and where the waste water goes TO. It's not just a municipal water pipeline in and a sewer line out as you will find in urban areas. Well water comes directly from the earth, goes through the house then back to the earth. The water cycle is quite incredible if you ask me.

In simplified terms, a water well is a hole drilled into the ground, say arbitrarily to 200' (60m for the new-schoolers), with a diameter of approximately 6" (there are variances with this and reasons for it, but we don't need to confuse things any more than they possibly already are). The well is drilled then cased with steel pipe at the surface, through the glacial till, overburden, rocks, clay, etc. Once the driller has gotten into potentially water-bearing formations (predominantly shale or sandstone), the piping is changed to pvc, known as the liner. The liner goes to the bottom of the well, with slots cut in it to allow the water to flow in from the "zone" (the aquifer). As the water fills the well, it will find its own level in the well and that is where the water level will generally stay when not being pumped. This is known as the "non-pumping static water level". This level could range from overflowing out the top of the well to barely above the "zone".

Arbitrarily, let's say the level is at 50' (15m) below grade. The submersible pump is installed and generally sits at a level close to the zone where the water is coming from the earth. The pump works in conjunction with the pressure system (usually in the basement mechanical room), and provides water for the home as needed. The water is tested for chemistry and bacteria, and treated as necessary to be the best that it can be for domestic use. This treatment will be discussed more in-depth later.

Well pumps last approximately 15-20 years. Again, quite an impressive feat considering that a pump provides water throughout the course of the day, every day... for 20 years or more! Some pumps that we have pulled and changed have been in the wells for over 30 years. There are many factors that can affect this: water quality, usage amount, quality of the pump, depth and horizontal distance. It is difficult to predict how long they will last, and usually when they give up the ghost, they just stop working without notice.

As a water well owner, there are added responsibilities that come with the home package in order to help keep your well healthy so it provides clean, pristine water for you and your family for many years. Well systems are relatively low-maintenance, but they should not simply be ignored until they fail or have a problem. Problems happen at any time but seem to prefer times like Christmas Eve, long weekends, etc. when all the relatives are in from out of town and water use is paramount. Not the best time to be out of water! It's best to try to keep up on its maintenance and take measures to avoid issues.

Simple maintenance can help extend the life of your pump and well system. The most common maintenance is to have your well **shock-chlorinated**. This process involves adding a large volume of chlorine-based solution (again, all wells and situations are different, but let's say 500 gallons of solution). Taps are run in the home until the chlorine is present.

Note: There are other solutions that are in use; hydrogen peroxide is another popular, effective chemical used, but chlorine-based solution is still the most common and is recommended by Alberta Environment.

Once the solution is at every tap, the solution is then left to just sit and work its magic. At this point, the chlorine has filled the well, is in the aquifer and all of the lines, the pressure tank, hot water tank and at each tap. This disinfects the system by killing bacteria and removing bio-fouling, algae, etc. that can grow in water systems.

After a period of approximately 24 hours, an outside tap is turned on (with a hose to get it out away from the house and away from nice lawns), and the chlorine is pumped out. After approximately three hours, the water should be running clear again with only minor residual chlorine odour. At this time, the taps inside the home can be opened up to clear the chlorine.

It is important to run the water ***outside first*** *in order to get as much chlorinated water outside as possible and a minimal amount into the septic tank.*

A vital component to a healthy septic system is the presence of bacteria. **Chlorine kills bacteria.** Chlorine is good for water wells but not good for septic systems.

Shock chlorination is a relatively inexpensive process which greatly helps keep your well and pumping system in good health. It is a helpful procedure to avoid problems which could become very large if ignored. Most of the well and system isn't visible to the naked eye, it is hidden deep below the surface of the earth. It is hard to see what's going on, but the chlorine treatments have been proven time and time again to help keep things healthy.

As with any infrastructure, water wells don't last forever. There are several factors which contribute to their sad demise. Most times when people have no water, it isn't necessarily that the well has reached the end of its life. Other things can happen as well. The most common issues and failures with wells are:

1. **Pumping system issues.** Most times when we get a call that a client is out of water, they are worried that the well has gone dry. This is almost never the case. Usually the pump has reached the end of its life and needs to be pulled and changed. Other electrical issues, pressure tank, etc. can also cause an out-of-water situation. Nine out of ten times they are a relatively straightforward fix. In extreme and rare cases, the aquifer for one reason or another just isn't producing any more water. In this case, a new well is required.

2. **Dirty water.** Sometimes water can get dirty suddenly then either stay that way or correct itself. There are contributing reasons for this:

   - The well could be very old
   - The well could be a low-producer and is being over-pumped
   - The aquifer may have changed
   - The casing could be letting in bad water due to a breach / perforation in the casing

There are many possible culprits, and thankfully there are just as many solutions. Perhaps the system needs a thorough cleaning (involving pulling the pump and flushing out the well using clean water and injecting air, blowing the contents up and out the top of the well). Perhaps the pump is too close to the bottom of the well and is sucking up sediment that has settled on the bottom. In this case, the pump can be raised and reset at a more effective depth, allowing for the sediments below the pump to settle out. There is almost always a solution, whether it be reducing the pumping rate to air-cleaning / flushing it, or in extreme cases, drilling a new well. Whatever the issues may be, the solutions are there.

3. The well may be very old and the casing may have deteriorated enough that it starts to let in bad water, bad water that the original driller cased off in order to keep out of the well itself. Lab testing and possibly putting a camera down the well can show if this has occurred. Some bad

water is extremely corrosive to the casing and can cause this failure to happen sooner than with other wells. If this is the case, most times a new replacement well has to be drilled.

As with many other relatively unknown and unfamiliar things, wells come with their own set of myths and misconceptions. One myth is that well water is not good for drinking – only showering, toilets, etc. There are many people who move to the country that continue to haul cumbersome 20 litre water bottles for their family to drink. The reality is that well water in most cases is very healthy. In fact, it is **as good or better than city water and most bottled waters.** They may require some simple filtration (reducing sodium or iron, etc.), but in most cases they are perfectly healthy as is. My own property has a well, and I find it very comforting that my drinking water does not have chlorine nor fluoride added to it.

In many cases, bottled water has been stripped of many of its valuable minerals. Then there is the whole ethical debate about drinking bottled water (and the displacement of said water from its aquifer source). Also, there are concerns of it sitting around in plastic bottles because by the time it is ingested it can be contaminated by the plastic container. A protected, private water well provides water straight from the earth. How can you beat that?

Another myth with wells is that if you drain the well, it will dry up permanently, requiring you to drill a new well.

People have accidentally left their taps on, watering the lawn for hours or days, and have called almost in tears, saying they have dried their well up. Not the case. Properly constructed wells are rigorously tested to confirm that they are, in fact, aquifers, which are basically streams flowing under the ground that are continually replenished with fresh water. If the well gets drained (it happens; for instance, if they are over pumped and the well is not a strong producer), in most cases, the well just needs some recovery time to fill up again and you are back in business.

Another myth concerning water systems is with cisterns. Cisterns are large holding tanks which store water. Often wells will trickle into the cistern, allowing large volumes of water to be available at any given time for the homeowners. The myth is that people would see a cistern and instantly think, 'Oh no, this place has no water'. That's not always the case. It is a proven fact that if wells are pumped 'lighter', less frequently, and are allowed recovery time, they are generally healthier and less prone to bacteria. Bacteria can flourish with the help of aerobic activities caused by the up and down movement of water in the column. A five gallon per minute (gpm) well is generally sufficient for domestic usage; however, a large home which has many feet of piping and a busy family who has high water demands, may notice that a five gpm system may not be sufficient at times. But, a five gpm well filling a cistern that has a 10 or 15 gpm pump will provide better pressure throughout this same home during peak demand. Cisterns involve an added cost and a minor amount of added maintenance (cleaning every year or two), but the benefits can be great.

As a well owner, there are small things you should do to help keep your water source protected and healthy. Things like making sure the casing is sticking up at least 30 cm (code) above grade. 50-80 cm is a good height as this allows the wellhead to usually be above the snow, easy to find for winter maintenance, and above snow melt, heavy rain, etc. Most E. coli bacteria issues occur when wells do not have proper caps or they are too close to the ground. Animals tend to try to make a well their new home only to plunge 200' to their deaths.

Make sure your well is sufficiently above grade and has a proper cap. It is also a good idea to have the ground slightly built up around it so water doesn't pool around the well.

As discussed, a shock-chlorination every couple of years is a good maintenance practice. While chlorinating, the system can be looked over as well in order to make sure that things are calibrated and running nicely. The water well and system are extremely important to the daily needs of your family and should be treated as such. It is important to keep it maintained and to routinely have the water quality tested. A sudden chemistry change or bacteria infiltration can go unnoticed and can signal issues with the system. A test will expose any contamination. If you, as the homeowner, are diligent in looking after your water source, it will provide you with years and years of pure, healthy water for you and your family.

Section Notes

What was my greatest take-away from this section?

What do I need to remember about this section?

32

Septic Systems

by Troy Niemans

As discussed in the chapter on water wells, if you own a rural property it is very likely that you also own a private septic system. If the wastewater from your home does not go out to a municipal sewer line, it is treated onsite by a septic system. This system, along with the water well, combines to create the biggest difference between rural and urban properties.

Being a septic owner comes with a list of responsibilities. There are different types of systems which are designed in accordance with:

- The house size
- The soil type
- The property parcel

- The presence of forest, as well as a host of other determining factors

In the end, all septic systems serve the same purpose: to treat the water and send it back into the earth, eventually finding its way back to the water table.

How does a system work? First of all, we start inside the home. All of the water fixtures – sinks, toilets, bath tubs, showers, laundry lines, etc. run via gravity, like fingers down to a main pipe that goes out under the floor of either the basement or crawl space. This line collects all of the solids and liquids then takes them out to the septic tank. The septic tank is a concrete or fibreglass (or in some cases pvc) vault that has a divider wall separating the tank into two chambers.

Disclaimer: There are several types of systems. Some are very advanced and/or alternative. Some have more than one tank, use bark mulch, or use different filters and aerator pumps.

There could be a whole book written about various septic systems, but for this chapter of this particular book, we will focus on the two most common treatment systems for the majority of residential properties, which are the **tank and field** and **mound** systems.

The common tank generally has concrete risers (manways) that come up from the top of the vault up to grade (surface level), allowing access for pumping out, monitoring and maintenance. Tanks average between 1000-3000 gallons in size. There is usually one manway for each chamber, or one manway which allows access to both chambers. Atop each concrete manway is a concrete lid. For safety reasons, the lids are very heavy. They are heavy so children can't lift them, wind doesn't blow them off, etc. The lids are taken off only when there is a good reason for it.

An alternative to the concrete risers is a material similar to hard plastic, known as ultrarib. This is a very strong composite which is more common with newer tanks and is excellent for keeping out surface water as they are virtually seamless. The lids for these are lighter (pvc), so they are held in place with four large stainless steel screws. Again, it takes effort to open them for the reason of safety. It is imperative that you as a landowner make sure that the lids are always on, are screwed down and are not damaged or broken.

The tank separates the liquids from the solids. All of the wastewater from the home pours into the first chamber of the tank, known as the working chamber. In the working chamber, bacteria eat and break down the solids, turning them into liquids and gases. The solids and greases, etc. settle on the tank bottom and float as well. This leaves the grey water in between, which flows up and over via a crossover tube, into the second chamber, called the dosing chamber. This second chamber should hold only grey water, no solids. The grey water is then sent out the to field via a pump or a syphon valve. It is very important that the second chamber does not fill with solids, or else the pump can become plugged. Also, solids sent to the field can plug it and cause serious damage. Invariably, some solids will float over to the second chamber, but for the most part if you look into the tank, the first chamber with be full of solids, the second chamber will be water.

The bacteria doesn't digest all of the tank contents, resulting in a sludge that settles on the bottom. The solids and undigested sludge and scum should be pumped out every couple of years (and to remove solids that may have crossed over into chamber two). The frequency of when to pump out the tank varies. It will depend on the number of occupants, the tank size and the tank condition. An average is every two to four years. When your system is pumped out, it is a good idea to have your pump truck operator have a look at the tank (from above) and give you an idea of the overall condition of things.

So, now that the solids and liquids are separated, what happens next? The liquids are sent out to the ground via a series of pipes, buried just below the ground surface.

There are thousands of fields in the ground, and the tank and field configuration is the proven old-school method of wastewater dispersal. In this type of system, the field comprises of a series of pvc pipes in the ground (with holes in them), that let the water out into the ground. A common configuration is to have a series of trenches, say two to three feet deep. These contain washed gravel on the trench bottom, then pipe on top of the gravel (commonly 4" diameter), with more gravel on and around this pipe. Geotextile cloth is then draped over this gravel to hinder sediments from trickling down into the gravel.

Once these layers of gravel, pipe, more gravel, and cloth are in place, they are covered over with native soil and loam, and then seeded to grass. The idea is that these trenches (known as laterals) will be barely visible and blend into the lawn. Usually, in the warmer months these are easily distinguishable as they will be greener and often more lush than the rest of the lawn since they are constantly being watered and nourished from within. In dry years, they are particularly noticeable. It is a good idea to keep an eye on the laterals, looking for things like consistent / even "greenness", indicating that the laterals are getting water evenly (and unlikely a line break nor root infiltration is occurring). If you suddenly start noticing that the ends or middle sections of a lateral are not greening like the rest, or water is surfacing somewhere, this could potentially be signalling an issue that should be looked into.

These laterals are designed to absorb and treat a certain amount of water per day, but they have a limit. It is therefore very important not to send out too much water as the risk of over-saturation can occur. This will be discussed later in this chapter.

The second chamber (aka dosing chamber or water chamber), is the chamber that either has a syphon valve or an electronic pump that sends the water out to the field. In the syphon system, once the water level reaches a certain height, the syphon kicks in and drains the water out (via gravity) to the field. At the field, there is a manifold or distribution box that effectively distributes the water out to the laterals then out to the earth. It is important that upon installation, the distribution is set up in such a way that all of the laterals get even amounts of water. This helps to ensure that some laterals aren't inundated with water, therefore prematurely over-saturating.

With an electronic pump configuration, a mechanical float completes the electrical circuit and sends power to the pump when the water level is high and the tank needs to be drained to the field. It then shuts off the pump when the level is low again. It is similar to syphon but it is electronic and doesn't necessarily rely on gravity. Both of these systems allow for an amount of time to pass between the "water sendings". This allows the ground time to deal with the water.

The new school…

There were several code changes to the standard of practice in 2009. Systems became pricier but they are also superior.

In the early days, as long as water went out into the ground it was considered good. That has changed. The water going out has to be treated by the soils in order to get it back to a useable and healthy state as it trickles back down into the groundwater system. Laterals on top of (for example) a natural gravel pit drains away quickly... but it doesn't treat the water well enough, so it is considered unacceptable. When a new system is designed and built, test pits are dug in the areas where the system will be. Samples of the different soils are sent to a laboratory. This lab analyzes the soil horizons and forms a report. Each type of soil has a mathematical number associated with it that allows designers and installers to know just how well the soil will treat the wastewater. This, along with the amount of bedrooms, fixtures, etc. help to determine just how many laterals (and how long they are) need to be installed in order to provide proper effluent treatment. Now, what if the ground is indeed gravel or sandstone? Or water is encountered at a shallow depth? None of these allow for a traditional in-ground field system.

We then have to install what is known as a sand mound, or simply a "mound". In a nutshell, a mound is a berm consisting of layers of aggregate that form an above ground field to treat the effluent. A common example of a mound would be 12 inches of washed concrete sand, approximately 5 feet wide, running 150 feet long. The sand just sits on the native ground. On top of the sand, we would find approximately 6 inches of washed gravel. On top of the washed gravel are a series of 1 inch pvc pipes that have small holes drilled into them, evenly spaced (arbitrarily let's say 2 feet apart). Usually the pipes form an "H" design. On top of the pipes is more gravel then the geotextile cloth. All of this is then covered over with loam to form a berm. The berm is tapered on the sides and ends, allowing the homeowner to mow it without difficulty once the grass has grown over it. It is important to seed the mound to allow grass to grow, rather than become a large weed patch. Once the grass has grown in, it is important to keep the mound mowed nicely as this helps it stay dry. Keeping fields and mounds dry help them function better as they have an easier time dealing with the water sent from the tank. An average mound is approximately 3-4 foot high in the middle.

By a large margin, most new systems are mounds. The washed sand is excellent and very effective in treating the wastewater. As it passes through the sand then down to the native ground, it has already been filtered and treated quite well. The native loam, etc. continues this treatment as the ground absorbs the water.

Whether you have a mound or a traditional field, you shouldn't drive anything heavy over them, nor plant anything other than grass on them. Just go over them with a lawn mower, a medium sized ride-on mower is generally okay.

While septic systems do last many, many years, they are not invincible. There are issues that can and will arise.

1. **The divider wall** in the tank is crucial to the septic system functionality. This wall, over time, can (and often will) deteriorate and essentially crumble from the top down. Eventually it can deteriorate enough that it will start allowing solids to flow over the wall into the second chamber. This is bad in that the solids can plug the pump and/or syphon, contributing to a potential backup. It can also cause solids to go out to the field or mound and plug it, which can cause an even bigger problem than a plugged or failed pump. It is a good idea to have a look at the wall yearly to make sure that it is in good enough shape and that it is separating the solids from the liquids. Some tanks are difficult to check and require a camera or entry, but even looking into the water chamber and confirming that there aren't a lot of solids floating in it is better than nothing. Some water is very corrosive to concrete and can escalate this type of failure. High salts, H2S and softener backwash can all contribute to this. Often the wall can be repaired if caught in time.

2. **Saturation**. If too much water is consistently sent to the field, this can saturate the ground and eventually the water will back up into the tank or possibly start coming out above ground. There can be many factors that can contribute to this. A leaking toilet can send out two to three times more water per day than the field can handle. This is very important to try to monitor and avoid. If you have a leaking toilet, it is wasting water and potentially taxing for your well – .5 gpm is 720 gallons per day! This can be

deadly to a septic system designed to absorb 500 gallons per day, especially when you add the 720 gpd to the already 300 gpd that is being treated just by normal usage, which totals 1020 gallons per day! Check for leaks and address them immediately. It is also a good practice to stagger your laundry throughout the week rather than doing seven loads on Saturday laundry day. Having a laundry day is taxing on the well and the septic system. Staggering it allows the ground absorption time. Also, your tank risers should come up above grade. This reduces surface water (rain, snow melt, etc.) from flowing into the tank (acting as a drain) and collecting all of this excess water and sending it to the field, saturating it. Keep it so that the only water entering the tank is from the house. Sometimes a saturated field can be dried out and saved with moderated usage, but saturating a field can also ruin it and become a huge expense. Be mindful of the water amounts.

3. **Roots in laterals**. Trees should not be planted near septic fields or mounds. The roots (especially poplars) will literally seek out these lush water sources and set up shop. The roots can infiltrate the piping and eventually plug them up to the point of total failure, with no water making it out to the ground. The roots can also break piping, etc. If there is root infiltration, they sometimes can be cleared out and laterals restored, but not always. Trees should be removed. If you see poplar "suckers" sprouting up around the field and tank area, eliminate them before they get too big.

Septic system myths... These can found in many shapes and sizes. A few common ones are:

1. **You must add bacterial additives / enzymes** to the tank so it works properly. Not true. There are enough enzymes and bacteria that we produce naturally that help the system function properly. Adding bacteria can actually create issues as it can form a gelatin-like material that can clog up pipes and pumps. There is enough bacteria in our day-to-day usage to keep systems functioning like they were designed to. Be careful what goes into your septic system, and don't flush garbage, food, feminine hygiene products, etc. A good general rule is to only flush down what goes through you, and toilet paper. And try to go easy on chemicals and cleaning products.

2. **Planting trees and gardens over the field is a good idea** as it is a great source of water and nutrients. False. Don't plant anything over the field (or near the tank) except for grass. Gardens are not good as it isn't wise to be tilling up and disturbing the soil above the field. Also, the chemicals and wastewater that the plants would absorb may not be healthy to ingest. Just grass. And keep it mowed.

3. **If it ain't broke, don't fix it!** False. Many people only think about the system when there is a problem, but maintaining it is an important part of homeownership. It should be treated like a car, in which you routinely

change the oil. You can save big dollars and costly repairs by simply having the tank pumped regularly, having a look inside at the divider wall, keeping trees away, keeping the grass mowed, checking for and stopping in-house leaks, annually checking the filter if there is one, etc. All of these small servicing suggestions will pay off greatly and save you money in the long run.

A private septic system is a wonderful thing to have. It sure beats having to haul all that wastewater away in a truck. Consider that with an average four-person family, the system treats and disposes of almost 100,000 gallons of wastewater annually. Incredible. With simple maintenance and care, your system should last for decades with relatively low operating costs. A textbook case of what you put into it, you'll get out of it.

Section Notes

What was my greatest take-away from this section?

What do I need to remember about this section?

33

Home Water Systems

by Troy Niemans

Water filtration and conditioning

The water your family consumes and uses on a daily basis really is the lifeblood of your property. For drinking, cooking, cleaning, and bathing, you want to ensure that you have healthy, clean water. For the most part, water wells do this naturally. A properly constructed well provides you with clean, cold water from within the earth's rock formations, which essentially are akin to naturally existing pipelines. Just as the depths and flow rates of wells can vary greatly, so can the quality. It isn't always ready to go as-is. Some water is very high in minerals, sodium, fluoride, etc. and some is simply cloudy with very fine sediment. Some has a very strong rotten egg odour, unpalatable to many people. There are many, many contributing factors and chemical combinations that can affect the water in a variety of ways.

The good thing is that in almost all cases, there are treatment solutions.

We've all heard of water softeners; they are very common in the foothills area since the water is often hard enough that, if left raw, it will scale appliances and damage hot water tanks. Water softeners are a very basic and common form of treatment. Softeners can also take out certain amounts of iron, if needed. If the iron amounts are too high and the softener can't fix it, a dedicated iron filter is needed. If minerals, sodium or nitrates are elevated, this can be remedied by reverse osmosis; a set of very fine disposable filters that reduce these levels by 80-90%. In the foothills area, softeners, iron filters and reverse osmosis filters are all very common fixtures in acreage homes (softeners in cities and town dwellings as well). To determine the necessary filtration, we always get a sample of the raw water to the lab for a detailed analysis. With the results in hand, we can interpret them and design conditioning solutions to address the issues presented by your raw water. The lab report is key.

There is often a mistake made where people just install a softener (for example) because they have heard that they simply need one. The thing is that it isn't uncommon for groundwater to be naturally soft. More commonly it is hard, yes, but there are plenty of farms and acreages that are on naturally soft water, negating the need for a softener. The lab report allows us to clearly know what the chemical make-up of the water is (average tests show 40-50 different components), showing the ppm concentrations of sodium, nitrates, sulphates, iron, total dissolved solids and fluoride, just to name a few. It also shows things like sodium adsorption ratio (SAR), which is important as this indicates how well plants can uptake and use the water. With a SAR value that is too high, you can water plants and grass as much as you want, day and night, and not see any result (or even kill the plant). Thanks to the miracles of modern science, treatment solutions have been invented to address almost all of the problematic water issues that surface.

A large part of what we do at Titan is to thoroughly test the water and septic systems for buyers when they are considering purchasing a property (or pre-testing systems for sellers prior to listing). We measure the flow of the well, explain the pros and cons, and help the buyer understand how much water the well is producing and how it will serve their daily needs. We also provide a complete lab analysis of the water. Once we receive the report from the lab, we go through it line-by-line to make sure it appears healthy, then we point out any red flags. There are set parameters and maximum concentrations as outlined by the Canadian Drinking Water Quality Guidelines to compare to. After we have interpreted and discussed the lab report, you will have a better understanding of how to read the report and will understand the makeup of your water. It is critical to know the potential filtration recommended, along with the costs of installation and yearly maintenance requirements.

The quality of groundwater varies greatly from well to well, and it isn't wise to assume water quality based on your neighbour's well. This brings us to some of the common mistakes that people make regarding groundwater and conditioning.

Top five rural water myths

1. **The neighbouring well is strong and very good tasting, so mine will be the same.** Studies show that, yes, there are connections between aquifers to varying degrees, sometimes an aquifer of bad water intermingles with an aquifer of good water. This can happen anywhere and at any depth. In a subdivision of say 16 homes all on their own well, you can find varying depth, flow rates and quality. One neighbour may have naturally beautiful, odourless, tasty water while across the fence his poor neighbour's water has such a high concentration of sulphides that you can smell the rotten eggs as soon as you walk in the door. Two wells 15 feet apart can yield completely different water.

2. **It's a water well; of course it needs a softener.** False. As touched on before, yes, it is common to need a softener, but not always. There are many aquifers that produce naturally soft water. If you are thinking about getting a softener, have the water tested and analyzed first. If you don't actually need to be buying and lugging

bags of salt down into your basement regularly (and this salt ending up in your septic system), why not find this out first?

3. **The water is clear, tastes okay and the people living there are still alive so the water must be fine.** False. The hardest stuff to filter out – things like nitrates, total dissolved solids, sodium, sulphates, fluoride, etc. are odourless and not detectable to the eye. The water can and usually does look crystal clear, but these elevated minerals and components can adversely affect health if left untreated. The only way to know is by analysis and interpretation.

4. **Shocking the well will fix everything.** Not true. Shock-chlorinating the well and system is very effective in treating bacteria and freshening up the water, eliminating iron bacterial sludge, bio-fouling and the associated odours, but the basal chemical makeup of the water is not generally affected by shocking the well. It doesn't eliminate sodium, solids, etc. and those values don't change after a shock. Is it a good practice to have the well shock-chlorinated? Absolutely. But it isn't the fix-all. It is an excellent way to clean things up, and if a problem (odour, for example) persists then we assess from there, after the fresh start.

5. **The rotten egg odour has always been there; it's just the way it is and can't be fixed.** It is interesting how

many times we've talked to rural property owners who have been putting up with stinky water for literally decades, thinking that it is simply non-fixable. There have been many times that we have installed a filtration unit for a client to rid the stinky odour, meanwhile they or the previous owners had struggled through it for 10, 20, 30 years prior, accepting that the water was unfixable. Again (and I know I'm repeating)... lab analysis. Assess, interpret and design a solution. With well water there is almost always a solution.

It is important to know the full picture when considering treatment.

- How much does the installation cost?
- How much maintenance will you as the landowner have to perform?
- How much will the maintenance costs be?
- For a system that uses water for backwashing / regenerating, how much water does this use and where does the wastewater go?
- Will it overtax my well?
- Does the backwash water go to the septic system?
- Can this overload the field?
- Will softener salts damage the tank and field?

These things should be discussed and considered to avoid surprises and costly future problems.

"Silt and sediment" in water may also require conditioning, and is one of the more tangible water issues. You can see the sediment. There are varied reasons for sediments in wells. Sometimes the aquifer has changed and is introducing silts or there may be a high amount of sludge in the well bore that is now falling into the water, mixing and creating discolouration. Perhaps the well casing has failed and is letting in soils. There are plenty of potential reasons. Installing a sediment filter (or series of them) can prove to be effective in stopping the silts from getting past the mechanical room, and not into your plumbing lines throughout the house. This is relatively cost-effective, but the maintenance amounts can vary greatly. You may find yourself changing filters weekly, monthly or yearly. Often, it is a good idea to try to get to the root and see if the sediment issue can be stopped in the well, before the water gets pumped to the house. This is where procedures such as pulling the pump and analyzing the well and system can be very constructive. We have pulled pumps that were literally sitting on the bottom of the well. We shortened the hose and wire, raising the pump 10 foot off the bottom of the well, allowing for a place for silt to settle. Voila, no more dirty water.

Other times, the well may be old or just has a lot of sediment that's accumulated over the previous 20 years. This is where a good air-lifting can have positive results, which is literally blowing out the well, removing sludge, silt, sediment and other treasures, and effectively bringing the well back to an almost new state. These procedures should be at least considered when dealing with dirty water. Filters are helpful, but if the problem can be stopped in the well, it is much better over the long run.

So, you've had your water analyzed and it came back showing a presence of bacteria. As you know by now, a shock-chlorination should be performed to fix the situation. But what if the bacteria keeps coming back? Or perhaps you just want better piece of mind that your family is protected. Ultraviolet sterilization is very effective for continuously eliminating bacteria. As the water passes by the UV bulb, bacteria is killed. This is a low-cost apparatus with very little maintenance, no chemicals and no backwashing. The bulb requires changing once a year (along with a quartz sleeve that keeps the bulb dry). Another way to keep bacteria at bay is to inject chlorine or other chemicals (i.e. peroxide) into the water continuously. This has been proven to be effective as well, but it can be more difficult to maintain and regulate the doses, and care should be used as it introduces chemicals to the house and septic system. It's effective but needs extra attention and monitoring.

When dealing with malodorous water, there are a variety of options, depending on the severity and concentration of the offending components. Usually, sulphides (h2s) in the water create this odour which produces the infamous rotten egg scent.

There are stand-alone units which eliminate the odour, usually utilizing catalytic carbon, greensand or other types of filtration. They range from chemical-free, using air to oxidize the h2s and iron, to using specific chemicals like potassium permanganate to help rid the water of sulphides. These systems resemble a softener in shape and size, and are generally also located in the mechanical room. They can handle a certain maximum amount of sulphides, but if the ppm concentration is too high, alternate methods need to be introduced. This is where chlorine or peroxide injection comes into play. As the water comes into the home, a pump administers a set amount of chlorine into the water stream. The water then generally sits in a holding tank (cistern or sealed tank) to allow for contact time. This contact time allows the h2s to be neutralized. The water then goes through a filter to eliminate residual chlorine, solids, remnants of the sulphides, etc. and then goes out to the piping throughout the home.

We touched on reverse osmosis (RO) earlier. By far, the most common RO configuration is a simple filter set which is generally mounted in the basement or under the kitchen sink. This provides purified drinking water through a dedicated tap, usually at the kitchen sink, fridge, wet bar, etc. This is a relatively low-cost system that produces beautiful drinking water. Another RO configuration is a whole-home system. This is a much larger apparatus that produces enough purified water to supply the entire house; all of the taps, hot water, showers and even the toilets. While this is effective in reducing contaminants and creating bottled water throughout the house, care should be exercised. These systems produce high amounts of wastewater in order to make the water good. They vary but can produce two to three times more wastewater than good water, which in most cases drains to your septic system. It is much better to have the wastewater go out to either a dry-well or dry creek bed. A dry-well typically is a small pit filled with gravel. The water goes here and dispenses out to the earth. These are favourable in that the sodium, contaminants and excess water don't go out to the septic system, potentially adding salts and overloading the system. Whole home RO systems create very nice water, but there should be a plan designed to deal with the wastewater.

i.e.: Your septic system is designed to handle a certain amount of daily water, say 400 gallons per day (gpd). If you indeed use 400 gallons per day, then if you are using whole home RO, this number shoots up to 800-1200 gpd (or more). This would eventually create septic issues if left unmitigated.

These are just a few common types of water treatment systems available. There are many solutions available that can help to improve your water and ultimately your quality of life. When considering filtration, have the water analyzed. The ensuing report will tell all, then solutions can be discussed, designed and installed.

Section Notes

What was my greatest take-away from this section?

What do I need to remember about this section?

Meet our contributing authors

Larry Metz

Meerkat Roofing and Exteriors LTD.

www.meerkatroofing.ca

MEERKAT ROOFING
& Exteriors
"We Go To Extreme Heights To Please You!"

James Lozinsky

James Lozinsky Prof Corp

www.JCL-LAW.ca

403-995-7744

JAMES C. LOZINSKY
LAWYER · MEDIATOR · ARBITRATOR

Shawna Roch

Shaw-Roco Solutions Inc.

www.shawrocosolutions.com

Shaw-Roco
Solutions Inc.

Julie Boake

Awedity Creative Inc.

www.aweditycreative.com

Bernice M. Winter,

A.C.C.I., F.C.C.I., President

Office: 403 509 2250

www.condo-check.com

condocheck®

Cory Alger

Southern Comfort Flooring

587-433-6893

coryalger@sc-flooring.com

https://www.sc-flooring.com

SOUTHERN COMFORT
FLOORING

Nathan Prins, A.L.S., S.L.S., P.Surv., B.Tech.
Alberta Land Surveyor (ALS)
Sovereign Geomatics Inc.
www.sovereigngeomatics.com

SOVEREIGN
GEOMATICS

Sandi Scott
Scott Mortgages
Cell: 403-333-8354
Email: sandi@scottmortgages.com
Website: www.scottmortgages.com
Facebook:
https://www.facebook.com/scottmortgages

QUANTUS
Mortgage Solutions

Troy Niemans
Titan Water and Septic
403-601-0811
https://www.titanwater.ca

TITAN RURAL WATER & SEPTIC SOLUTIONS TITANWATER.CA

About the Author

Mark E. Meincke

RE/MAX Signature Properties

403-463-4313

mark_meincke@yahoo.ca

Shortly after graduating high school, Mark's need to make a difference and help others led him to the military. With the Gulf War happening, Mark felt the best way for him to contribute to his community, was to serve his country as best as he could. Though there were many military trades to choose from, Mark chose the most difficult path possible, and joined as an infantry soldier. He felt that if he was going to join, then there were not going to be any half measures, so he jumped in with both feet.

Although the infantry wasn't a great fit for Mark's compassionate personality, it did provide him with a sense of accomplishment, and confidence which he still carries with him today. After returning home from an United Nations Peacekeeping tour of duty in Croatia, Mark decided to leave the military and go to college. After trying a few different career paths, Mark unexpectedly found himself building a Real Estate business.

His natural charisma and helpful nature quickly earned the trust and loyalty of his clients. By his third year in business, Mark was finding success and fulfilment as a Realtor, though there was still something missing. With the birth of his first son, Cole, Mark was compelled to share his favorite life lessons by writing his first book, "Why not Me?" In 2008, shortly after the birth of his youngest son Dawson, the book was published, and won an international literary award for it's contributions to human potential. Mark's passion for sharing wisdom through writing has continued on by publishing dozens of articles on LinkedIn, and now by the creation of the Home Seller's Bible, for owners, agents, and investors.

Mark now lives in the beautiful foothills of southern Alberta with his amazing wife Tracey, his two boys, and three step children.